D. H. LAWRENCE

D. H. LAWRENCE

A Personal Record

by

E. T.

CAMBRIDGE UNIVERSITY PRESS

Cambridge

London   New York   New Rochelle
Melbourne   Sydney

Published by the Press Syndicate of the University of Cambridge
The Pitt Building, Trumpington Street, Cambridge CB2 IRP
32 East 57th Street, New York, NY 10022, USA
296 Beaconsfield Parade, Middle Park, Melbourne 3206, Australia

First published by Jonathan Cape Limited 1935
This paperback edition first published by the
Cambridge University Press 1980

First printed in Great Britain at the Alden Press, Oxford
Reprinted in Great Britain at the
University Press, Cambridge

British Library Cataloguing in Publication Data

Chambers, Jessie
D. H. Lawrence.
1. Lawrence, David Herbert – Biography – Youth
2. Authors, English – 20th century –Biography – Youth
823'.9'12   PR6023.A93Z/   80–40254

ISBN 0 521 29919 5

CONTENTS

NOTE

THE author of this book is referred to by D. H. Lawrence in his *Autobiographical Sketch* as 'the girl who had been the chief friend of my youth'. Very gracefully he acknowledges his indebtedness to her by saying that she launched him on his literary career 'like a princess cutting a thread, launching a ship'. At a much earlier date he had created the fictitious Miriam on the basis of their relationship, and an account of the circumstances which gave rise to *Sons and Lovers* are to be found in the following pages. 'E. T.' has here set down her recollections of this early friendship, and the story has involved a vivid and detailed picture of Lawrence's life during the formative years of adolescence and early manhood. The portrait is unique, as was the intimate knowledge of Lawrence at the time, and many important details of his upbringing and education are here given which but for this personal record must have remained unknown. The narrative is of an early friendship, in many ways idyllic, which suffered shipwreck for reasons beyond the control of the protagonists. Its value lies not only in the convincing portrait of the youthful Lawrence but in the sincerity, reticence and imaginative understanding implicit in the telling.

M. P.

Parts of the chapters on Student Days, Literary Formation, and Literary Début have appeared in *The European Quarterly* and are reprinted by courtesy of the editors.

D. H. LAWRENCE

à avia
Herbert

FAMILY LIFE

My first clear recollection of D. H. Lawrence goes back to the Congregational Sunday School at Eastwood which we both attended. On a Sunday afternoon in each month the superintendent used to organize recitations instead of the usual lessons. We were sitting in groups, each with a teacher, the boys on one side of the long room, the girls on the other. The little dais at the end where the superintendent stood seemed far away, and the poems were seldom worth listening to, so that when a slight, fair boy of about eleven mounted the platform, my attention was only attracted when it became evident that he could not remember the beginning of his poem. He stood nervous and alert, the perfect pattern of a scholarship boy, and whispers went round that it was 'Bert Lawrence'. His elder sister E. was sitting near the platform, giggling at his distress. He opened his lips several times, only to find that the words would not come. The room grew ominously still. The white-haired, rosy-cheeked superintendent smiled encouragement, and Lawrence's sister giggled hysterically. At last the boy turned a tortured face to the superintendent and made a request, which was granted by a cordial nod. Lawrence thereupon drew a sheet of note-paper from the inside pocket of his coat, glanced at it, then recited the poem correctly, and got down from the platform with a white face.

In all probability I should never have become acquainted with Lawrence but that his mother and mine struck up a sudden friendship one Sunday evening after chapel. They found themselves together in the porch, glanced at one another, smiled, and walked out side by side. My mother was more of a stranger to the mining country than Mrs. Lawrence, having lived there only some five or six years to Mrs. Lawrence's twenty. A mysterious affinity drew them together, and they had a heart to heart talk. At least Mrs. Lawrence told my mother all her family troubles. I have a dim recollection of mother being very late home from chapel, and on going to look for her in the lane, seeing the two small figures dressed in black, and Mrs. Lawrence talking with animation.

My grandparents had been staunch chapel people all their lives, and their pew in the Congregational chapel was in the same aisle as the Lawrences', only across the gangway. Old-fashioned Eastwood people, however, did not speak of the Congregational chapel but referred to it as 'Butty's Lump'. The promoters of the scheme for building the new chapel were influential at the colliery, and the surest means of securing a good 'stall' in the pit was to make a handsome donation to the building fund. Perhaps that explains why our chapel had its air of elegance, so rare

in nonconformist chapels. The Sunday School consisted of the gloomy rooms of the British School where
Lawrence served his apprenticeship as a pupil-teacher.

Mr. Remington 'with his round white beard and his
ferocity', was my teacher as he was Lawrence's, though
we were not in the class at the same time. The old
man would stand in front of us, clapping his hands to
the tune and singing with us:

> Sound the battle cry
> See the foe is nigh
> Raise the standard high
> For the Lord,

his old voice making a harsh dissonance with our shrill
young ones. Instructing us in Sabbath observance
Mr. Remington said he always 'shulled' the peas on
Saturday night.

The charming young Welshman who was the
minister at that time was a great friend of our family.
He and father used to have long and animated
discussions about the authenticity of the Bible. The
minister offended mother when he said in his bright
way that the story of the Garden of Eden was just a
beautiful fairy-tale to explain the beginnings of life
on earth to simple people. Mother protested with
warmth:

'If you will doubt one part of the Bible you will
doubt all', and thereafter went to bed, leaving the men
to discuss the Bible until the small hours.

At that time father was an active member of the Christian Endeavour class and would sometimes stay up until two in the morning preparing a paper when it was his turn to give an address. He always tried to make it homely and drew his illustrations from incidents within his own experience. He would talk about it for days beforehand, explaining the various points to mother, and we children in the bedroom above the kitchen used to hear him earnestly rehearsing his prayer. Mother was sceptical about all this. She would have liked father to see life steadily and see it whole. But father was not built that way. Life for him was a patchwork.

It was about this time that father read *Tess of the D'Urbervilles* to mother from the *Nottinghamshire Guardian*, in which it appeared as a serial story. I was aware of the thrill of anticipation on Saturday afternoons, but I could not understand why he should be reading the newspaper aloud for such a long time (for we youngsters were not allowed to speak while father was reading to mother), nor why mother was flushed and excited, and kept making little exclamations of surprise and dismay. I would stand on a low stool behind father's armchair to see how much more he had to read, but could make nothing of the dull-looking columns of print.

We were not directly acquainted with the Lawrence children in those days but I heard their names mentioned from time to time. Father had seen E. trespassing in our mowing grass and came home very angry.

'That eldest lass of Lawrence's is brazen soft,' he said to mother. 'When I shouted to her to get out she just stood and sauced me. I s'll tell her mother.'

Ernest Lawrence was already a legendary figure. He had a post in a shipping office in London, we understood, and earned a handsome salary. He it was who kept his mother supplied with the good quality gloves and boots that had attracted my mother's attention when she had first noticed Mrs. Lawrence in the procession of colliers' wives that used to stream past our cottage on Friday afternoons, on their way to the colliery offices to draw the men's pay. He was quite the fairy prince of the family, but a chance remark of father's stuck in my mind:

'I never see such a young fool in my life as that lad of Lawrence's, Ernest, do they call him. There I met him walking down the street in a top hat, frock coat, and yellow kid gloves.'

I heard the irony in mother's laugh.

'How weak-minded,' she said.

On the one occasion when I saw Lawrence's father in those early days I had a momentary impression of richness and warmth, both of colouring and voice. He seemed to be a man of medium height with ruddy cheeks and black hair and whiskers. I have been told that as a young man he was fine looking, and wore a handsome black beard. He was also a first-rate work-man, and was invariably called upon when there was a particularly difficult job to be done in the pit. The story goes that once when he was having his hair cut, the barber left him after doing one side, and turned to shave a customer who was waiting with chin lathered, whereupon Mr. Lawrence got up in a huff and went off to another barber.

I was eleven when we left the cottage my father always referred to as 'the old hom'stead', and went to live at the little farm some three miles farther into the country. The farm was about a mile from the nearest village, and even the cart road ended at our yard-gate. The house was long, and the line of the roof was broken by a gable window which matched the porch over the front door. The farm buildings adjoined the house and formed one side of a square. The front garden lay snugly in the angle between the house and our neighbour's high yard-wall and buildings. From the front door we looked down the length of garden which was fenced off from the crew-yard, over a croft and into the wood that shut us in completely on the west. The big yard-gate and the two small gates into the garden were painted cream, 'Queen Anne's White' the estate painters called it, to match the cream of the window frames. At the back of the house was a big garden divided from the stackyard by railings, con-taining two fine cherry trees with a low spreading apple tree between them, several plum trees, and currant and gooseberry bushes. Beyond was a rough grass plot with an apple tree in the centre and clumps of daffodils in the hedgebottom.

From the stackyard the land dipped to the valley where we could see in the hollow the red roofs of Felley Mill, and away on the right Moorgreen reservoir gleaming like tarnished silver. In the valley bottom the two brooks that drained the mill-pond into the reservoir ran over the road and were crossed by stepping stones, while the shaggy expanse of the Annesley Hills, dotted with patches of woodland, rose steeply behind. Further to the right, High Park wood covered the hills above the lake, and among the trees we could see the little tower of the shooting lodge which Lawrence was to make the scene of his first novel. Our orchard was an irregular triangle cut out of the wood, and across the width of two fields was a nursery of young firs and spruce trees we called the Warren. We had a right of way through the Warren and across the meadow which brought us to the high road just above the reservoir, and this was the path Lawrence usually took when he came to see us.

There was talk of Mrs. Lawrence paying us a visit when first we went to live at the farm, but we had been there three years before she came. Eventually father told Lawrence how to find the field path and the way through the Warren, and so bring his mother by the short cut. It was on a day in early summer when the small, vigorous woman, and the slender boy she called Bertie, came into the farmyard, so still in the afternoon sunshine. Mother went out to greet them, and as she took them into the parlour, Mrs. Lawrence, complaining of the heat, said in her crisp way:

'I'm thankful you haven't got a fire in here.'

We sat down to an early tea before the rest of the family came in. I had to go into the kitchen to boil eggs, and was surprised when the tall, fair boy followed me, and stood silently looking about him in a curious, intent way. The new staircase that had been put in for us made a big bulge on one wall, with deep recesses at either end. The recess beside the fireplace had a little window looking into the back garden. Lawrence seemed to be taking everything in with his eyes. It made me feel uncomfortable to see the peculiarities of our kitchen subjected to such keen scrutiny.

When tea was over we went out of doors. Mrs. Lawrence and mother moved away together, talking the incomprehensible talk of adults. Already I felt that Mrs. Lawrence pitied mother on account of her big family, and for living in such a queer, out-of-the-way spot. There was a tinge of patronage in her voice.

Lawrence and I went into the field beyond the stackyard. He stood quite still there, as if fascinated with the view of the Annesley Hills and High Park wood, with the reservoir gleaming below.

The single point of interest he had for me lay in the fact that he was still a schoolboy, as his Eton coat and collar reminded me. My own schooling, which had been of the crudest, had finished six months before, and my lack of education was a bitter humiliation to me. I was aware that this rather aloof youth had been for some years at the High School, and that he had studied French and German. I fancied that his superior education enabled him to appreciate things which were inaccessible to me. It was with a sense of getting even with him that I asked him abruptly how old he was.

'Fifteen,' he replied with a quick glance.

'I thought so. I'm fourteen,' I responded, aware that my question had been uncivil.

'You go to school?' I continued.

'Yes, to the High,' he answered, and gave me no further information.

'I don't care for the name of Bertie,' I went on, with a vague feeling of hostility. 'It's a girlish name. Do they call you Bertie at school?'

'No, of course not. They call me Lawrence.'

'That's nicer, I think. I'd rather call you Lawrence.'

'Do call me Lawrence,' he replied quickly, 'I'd like it better.'

He was shy and withdrawn, as if taking in many impressions at once. I felt that I was lacking in courtesy towards him, but I was terribly afraid this High School boy might look down on me.

Merely to prove my independence I set out a little

later to visit a friend who lived on the opposite side of the wood. At the door I ran into Lawrence. His penetrating glance went over my hat, my face, my cloak.

'Are you going out?' he asked, disapproval in his voice. He had been exploring the farm with my brothers and his face glowed with excitement. He was naturally pale, but the keenness of his glance and his swiftly changing expression made him seem vivid. I told him where I was going, and he asked excitedly:

'How do you get there? Which way do you go?'

'Through the wood,' I replied.

'You go through there?' he said eagerly, nodding towards the wood.

When I returned everybody was crowded in the kitchen and the conversation had turned upon books. My parents adored Barrie, *The Little Minister* and *A Window in Thrums*. The talk was lively and Mrs. Lawrence seemed to be the pivot upon which the liveliness centred. She struck me as a bright, vivacious little woman, full of vitality, and amusingly emphatic in her way of speaking. Her face changed rapidly as she talked and she had a habit of driving home her views with vigorous shakes of the head. She took a keen interest in things around her. As she said of herself, she entered into her children's pursuits and kept young through them. The conversation was mainly between Mrs. Lawrence, father, and my elder sister, with Lawrence joining in occasionally. I listened for awhile in silence, then ventured to mention my favourite author.

'Who likes Scott?' I asked.

'*I* do,' Mrs. Lawrence replied, beaming encouragement upon me.

After this visit Lawrence came to the farm nearly always on his mid-week half-holiday. He would step quietly into the kitchen, often bringing some magazine or other to our book-loving household. He seemed gentle and reserved, and talked chiefly to my father, who liked him. He was rather slow at making friends with my brothers, and we on our side were shy of him, and afraid lest he should give himself airs. I have no particular recollection of Lawrence during that first summer except as a quiet presence coming suddenly out of the sunshine into the kitchen, warm with the fragrance of baking bread. Father and he seemed to find a good deal in common, and I noticed from the first that father talked to him almost as if he were grown up. I remember hearing them discuss whether it was possible to store electricity, and father spoke as if he expected Lawrence to know all about it. Occasionally he would bring a copy of *Black and White* and they would talk about the illustrations, and I heard Lawrence describe the method of reproduction. These discussions introduced an interesting variety into our somewhat uneventful days.

Lawrence's schooldays finished that summer and he became a clerk in a Nottingham warehouse. We saw rather less of him then, but I heard him tell mother, in a voice that was clearly an unconscious imitation of his mother's, how Ernest and his fiancée had spent a fortnight's holiday with them, and that it had proved something of a strain. In October Ernest paid a flying visit to Goose Fair, and the next week we heard that he was dangerously ill in London and his parents had been summoned to his bedside. Almost immediately afterwards came news of his death, and we felt stunned by the tragedy. His mother had him brought home and buried in the cemetery at New Eastwood. She told my mother later, that when she reached her son's bedside she could scarcely recognize him, his head and face were so swollen and inflamed. He had returned to London in the raw morning hours after an exhausting week-end, and she could only think that he had caught a chill which brought on the fatal erysipelas. Telling me about this tragic journey years later she said:

'Yes, and I had to do everything myself, find out about the trains and how to get to Ernest's lodgings. His father was with me but he was no help; he stood just as if he was dazed.'

Only a few weeks after Ernest's death father came home from the milk-round with more bad news. It was Bertie this time, down with pneumonia. Mother looked stricken.

'I don't know whatever Mrs. Lawrence will do if that son's taken from her,' she said. 'She told me when she was here with him that however much she loved

Ernest it was nothing to what she felt for the one she brought with her. He had always meant more to her than any of the others.'

The trouble in the Lawrence family cast a gloom over our household, and mother inquired anxiously every day for news. It seemed a long time before father brought word that the patient was out of danger. His mother's nursing had saved his life, was the general verdict. When he was convalescent he began to send messages by father, begging one of us to go and see him. My sister took him a bunch of snowdrops that grew beneath the parlour window. She told us how gay he was, and how keenly he was looking forward to coming to The Haggs again, as soon as he was strong enough. His mother said he had grown so much in bed, she was sure his suits would all be too short for him.

On a day in early spring father brought him along in the milk-float. Mother and I watched from the kitchen window as the tall, thin youth in a dark over-coat stepped down from the float and walked slowly up the garden path.

'How white he is, how thin, poor lad,' mother was saying. He came into the kitchen, frail but eager, delighted to be with us again. Father seemed equally delighted. I do not know why my parents loved Law-rence as they did, but they were as glad at his recovery as if he had been their own son. They told him he was to come up just when he liked.

'Come up through the Warren, Bert,' father said. 'You want to get the smell o' them pine trees into your lungs. They're reckoned to be good for weak chests, aren't they? Take deep breaths and get your lungs full of the scent.'

From then his visits were a matter of course, and he became almost one of the family. He told us rather shamefacedly that his mother said he might as well pack his things and come and live with us. In later years he said that in those days he was only happy when he was either at The Haggs or on the way there. He vastly enjoyed the freedom of his long convalescence, and spent a month at Skegness with an aunt who kept a 'select' boarding-house on the front. He sent long descriptive letters to the family in general, in one of which he said that he could stand in his aunt's drawing-room and watch the tide rolling in through the window. My sister wrote back at once and said what an uncomfortable drawing-room his aunt's must be, with the tide rolling in through the window! He came home quite strong, and I heard father say what a rare good lad Bert was to his mother. He would blacklead the grate and scrub the floor. Lawrence told me himself that he never minded father seeing him with a coarse apron tied round his waist, but if he heard my brother's step in the entry he whipped it off on the instant, fearing he would despise him for doing housework.

At that period I was in a state of furious discontent and rebellion. I was the family drudge and hated it.

My lack of education was a constant humiliation. The desire for knowledge and a longing for beauty tortured me. I came to the conclusion that unless I could achieve some degree of education I had better never have been born. I quarrelled continually with my brothers, who tried to order me about. I felt an Ishmael, with my hand against everybody, and everybody's hand against me. I did not know that Lawrence was aware of my state of mind, but one day he suddenly took an end of chalk from his pocket and wrote on the stable door:

Nil desperandum.

'What does it mean?' I asked, although I knew.

'Never despair,' he replied, with an enigmatic smile, and ran away.

Eventually I succeeded in making myself so disagreeable that mother in desperation sent me back to school and I became a pupil-teacher. Then began an arduous life of studying, teaching, and helping with the housework, which still somehow left time for the most exciting games.

It was by now an established rule that Lawrence should come to tea on a Saturday, and when he entered the house he brought a holiday atmosphere with him. It was not merely that we were all nice with him, he knew how to make us nicer to one another. Even my eldest brother thawed when Lawrence was there. He brought a pack of cards, and taught us whist, and we played fast and furious, with the younger children crowding round to watch, and Lawrence excitedly scolding and correcting us. When he was in the mood he could be very funny, particularly when mimicking the members of the Christian Endeavour class repeating in turn 'The servant of the Lord is like a well-filled house . . .' He used to say that our laughter was Homeric. He would have us dance in our little kitchen, and once while we paused for breath he said:

'Father says one ought to be able to dance on a three-penny bit.'

He seldom spoke of his father and we at once exclaimed:

'Why, does your father dance?'

'He used to, when he was a young man. He ran a dancing class at one time,' he replied briefly.

It seemed unbelievable; we had never thought of his father in that light.

Lawrence was extraordinarily kind and willing to help with whatever task was afoot. He was most considerate towards mother, with her big, unruly family, so hard to manage, each of us at a different stage of development, each making a different demand upon her. Several times when he came in and found her with more to do than she could get through he fetched water for the boiler, tidied up the hearth, and made a fire in the parlour where my sister (who was also a pupil-teacher) and I did our lessons. And I well remember a basket of tiny pickling onions that stood on the stone slab outside the back door for weeks, waiting to be peeled.

They suddenly disappeared, and mother said that Bert had peeled them; he just sat down and did them without saying a word to anyone. No task seemed dull or monotonous to him. He brought such vitality to the doing that he transformed it into something creative.

It was the same at harvest time. Lawrence would spend whole days working with my father and brothers in the fields at Greasley. These fields lay four miles away, and we used to pack a big basket of provisions to last all day, so that hay harvest had a picnic flavour. Father enjoyed Lawrence's company quite as much as the rest of us. There was for years a fine understanding between them, a sympathy and recognition of what was best in each other. I heard father say to mother:

'Work goes like fun when Bert's there, it's no trouble at all to keep them going.'

It was true; in those early days Lawrence seemed so happy that merely to be alive and walking about was an adventure, and his gift for creating an atmosphere of good fellowship made work a joy. One could not help being affected by his vitality and charm. Mother made a remark that set me speculating. She said:

'I should like to be next to Bert in heaven.'

I did hope heaven wouldn't turn out to be a sort of eternal Sunday school. Our ideas of heaven must have been remarkably concrete, for Mrs. Lawrence told mother that she looked forward more to meeting her son Ernest in heaven than Jesus Christ Himself.

Lawrence's speech abounded in vivid and oddly

characteristic turns. I remember hearing him say in his blithe way:

'Ah, there's a custard for dinner, it rejoiceth my heart to see.' If he wanted a small piece of cake he would say in his rather high-pitched voice, 'Only give me a smeggin.' Anything he didn't like was 'a measly thing' and an inferior thing 'wasn't a patch' on something else. He amused us mightily by showing us how a girl acquaintance laughed. He would open his mouth wide and emit a sudden explosive giggle that was so comically like the original we laughed to exhaustion. He told us the story of his father bringing home a whole ham and then stopping payment for it each week out of the housekeeping money.

'Mother carried on about it week after week,' said Lawrence, with a touch of pained recollection in his voice. 'At last father could stand it no longer, and when mother began again he turned and looked at her, "Woman, how'd tha feeace" he said, and I nearly felt sorry for him.'

We laughed uproariously, and Lawrence laughed too, a little ruefully.

'And did she stop then?' we asked.

'Oh, yes,' he said, 'even mother had to laugh.'

I had been a pupil-teacher fifteen months before I received my first wages — five golden sovereigns. To celebrate the occasion I invited Lawrence to tea, and he agreed to come on a school day. It was sultry July weather and when I came home mother had laid tea at one end of the long parlour-table. Lawrence had not arrived, and we thought he might have one of the bad headaches to which he was subject just then. He told us that when he had a headache he was usually flushed and people would tell him how well he was looking, and he never contradicted them. At last we saw his dark slim figure emerging from the Warren, and he came in looking pale and tired, for like myself he had spent the day in school. We had tea in the cool parlour, mother, the two small children, Lawrence and myself, the rest of the family being away in the hay fields.

It was my eldest brother's twenty-first birthday and Lawrence seemed to yearn for his friendship. He had brought presents — a picture 'Colt-hunting in the New Forest', from himself, and a necktie, accompanied by a note of platitudinous greeting, from his mother. We admired the presents, and I noticed Lawrence's half-apologetic gesture as he handed the note to my mother, and her faint irony, like a mental grimace, on reading it.

After tea we went into the wood. I particularly wanted to show him a colony of tall foxgloves I had come across. The wood held a fascination for us. The shade, the murmur of the trees, the sense of adventure, the strong odour of the undergrowth, the sudden startled call of a pheasant, the whirr of a partridge's wings, were thrilling things. The gamekeepers must often have seen us, but we never saw them, and in all our wanderings about the wood no gamekeeper ever made himself visible to us. The flowers in their seasons were exciting events, first, anemones while the trees were still bare and cold, their pale flowers nearly hidden in their green frills, then celandines, and purple unscented violets in the lush grass of the ridings, and later the paths misty with forget-me-nots, and the miracle of the bluebells that made a blue carpet under the trees and filled the air with an intoxicating odour. We used to gather armfuls that lay heavy like sheaves of corn, only for their waxen coldness and penetrating fragrance. There seemed no flower nor even weed whose name and qualities Lawrence did not know. At first I was sceptical of his knowledge.

'How do you know what it is?' I asked him.

'I *do* know,' he replied.

'But *how* do you know? You may be wrong,' I persisted.

'I know *because* I know. How dare you ask me how I know,' he answered with heat.

I led him to where the foxgloves stood, like Red Indian braves, I said. He gave them that intense glance I was now so accustomed to I scarcely noticed it, and said nothing, and I thought he disliked my simile.

For a long time I was reluctant to go to his home, and Lawrence said reproachfully:

'I know why you won't come; it's because of father.'

I hastened to reassure him, but indeed I had heard

that his father sometimes got drunk, and in my childhood a drunken man had been a thing of terror.

'There's nothing for you to be afraid of,' Lawrence
went on. 'You'd never see him, he's hardly ever in.'

And so I found it to be. One rarely saw Lawrence's
father. When he had washed and changed into his
'shifting' clothes he went out to join his cronies in the
public-house.

The family was living then in what Lawrence called
'Bleak House', because it stood so open to the winds.
They had a wide view over the houses in the valley to
the meadows beyond, and to where High Park wood
began. Lawrence has told me how he used to watch
the cloud shadows stalking across the fields.

I did not go to the Lawrences' house many times
before I became aware of a curious atmosphere such as
I had never known before. There seemed to be a tightness in the air, as if something unusual might happen
at any minute. It was somehow exciting, yet it made
me feel a little sick. I thought for a long time that it
was the memory of Ernest's tragic death, and of the
mother's heroic fight for the life of her younger son, that
was the cause of the strung-up feeling in their household. It was not due specifically to anything that was
said or done, although happenings there had sharp
edges and a dramatic quality that made them stand out
in one's memory. It was a constant quality, something
one felt immediately on entering the house. I liked to
go, just to feel, as it were, or to listen to the curious,

powerful vibration, so different from our house, or any house I have ever known. Perhaps it was the strong emotional tension between mother and son, and in a directly contrary sense, between husband and wife, and father and son, that made the strangely vibrating atmosphere.

Mrs. Lawrence, though small, was an arresting figure with shrewd grey eyes in a pale face, and light-coloured hair. Her smallness was more than compensated for by her vigour and determination. All her energy was expended upon her children, who adored her; she was such a contrast to the poor, disinherited father. She was an excellent housewife and a kind neighbour to the motherless girls who lived near. Her confidence in herself and her pronouncements upon people and things excited my wonder. It was new to me to meet anyone so certain of herself and of her own rightness. But she could be vivid in speech, gay and amusing; and in spite of a keen edge to her tongue, she was warm-hearted. She said quite frankly that she was interested mainly in her sons. My mother used to say that she was always sorry to have a girl-child, because of the difficulties inherent in a woman's life. But Mrs. Lawrence's attitude was something different.

A curious feature of the Lawrence household was the way in which various girls would drift in casually, stay and talk a little, and then go as casually as they came. Lawrence became a pupil-teacher about a year after his illness, and he would sit at the table doing his lessons, not in the least put out by the conversation going on around him. In those leisurely days we had the pleasant habit of going to meet one another, and if several of our family were going to the Lawrences' to tea, Bert would come to meet us, accompanied by several girls. His mother used to smile and say there was safety in numbers. Speaking of her eldest son who had been married some years, she said in her emphatic way:

'Yes, and *he* was never going to leave me. "I shall always stop with you, mother, and take care of you," he used to say. And at seventeen he was arming a girl round.'

Mrs. Lawrence spoke with such comical emphasis we couldn't help laughing, but there was a thrust behind her words.

Another time she said in a curious tone of half-comic, half-bitter reminiscence:

'Ay, our Ern once heard E. asking me if I was pretty when I was a girl. "Were you pretty, our mother, when you were a girl?" she said. And Ern turned on her: "Pretty?" he said, "*Of course* she was pretty, a long sight prettier than you'll ever be, don't you worry." That was what our Ern said, "*Of course* she was pretty." '

Lawrence told us one winter that a flourishing pork-butcher in Eastwood wanted him to make out the bills in his shop from seven till nine on Friday evenings. He was to get five shillings for the two hours, and he felt he ought not to refuse. There was a note of dread in his voice. 'Oh, Bert, you'll smell of pork,' mother said. My sister laughed and said she would come and look at him through the shop window. It seemed shocking to me, and I said nothing. Lawrence turned to me. '*You* come and look at me,' he said. 'You *will* come, won't you?' I saw him one evening, a strangely isolated figure in the busy shop, industriously keeping accounts. It pained me to see him, and I was turning away in shame, when he suddenly caught sight of me, and instantly came out to speak to me. He knew quite well how I felt. 'If you can wait until nine I can walk home with you,' he said. But I couldn't wait until nine. Lawrence gave the job up soon afterwards.

When Lawrence discovered that we had never seen the sea, he persuaded mother to let us go on a day trip to Skegness. His own intense enjoyment gave a keener edge to our pleasure. He knew all the landmarks on the way, and would not let us miss a single point of interest. We had to rush to the carriage window to observe the graceful lines of Gedling Church spire rising sheer out of the valley. Further on there was Bottesford Church with its handsome dog-toothed ornament, and we tried to descry the outline of Belvoir Castle standing high on its ridge. At Boston we craned our necks to catch a glimpse of the famous Stump dominating the fens with its sombre dignity. But it was more than merely *seeing* these landmarks; it was a kind of immediate possession, as though to have missed seeing them would have been to lose an essential moment of life. An outing with Lawrence was a memorable experience. There was a sense of immediacy; each moment as it came seemed to be a culminating point of existence. His face, and particularly his eyes, were alight with eagerness that we should miss nothing of what stirred his own delight so deeply.

At the seaside we found a greyish day, and I saw that what mattered was not the colour of the sea, about which I had wondered so much, but the expanse, and the wide horizon, and the quite different quality of light. We paddled, and dried our feet in the sand, and A. called in her tone of conscious ownership to her brother to dry her feet for her. He made a gesture of protest, but obeyed all the same, kneeling and dusting the sand from her feet with his handkerchief. We ate our lunch on the beach, and after tea, which we had in a café, went to buy presents to take home. As Lawrence was the only one of us who had tasted melon he bought one and we retired into an arbour in the public gardens to eat it. He assured us it would be delicious, and cut it into half a dozen strips. Mine tasted like turnip, and was quite as hard. But that was a secondary consideration; we had eaten melon; it was an experience the more. Lawrence had a knack of describing where he had been and what he had done in such a way as to make one feel that the thing he had seen was one of the few things in the world really worth seeing, and what he had done was just what any vitally alive person would want to do. But he was apologetic about the melon; the one he had tasted previously really had been delicious — this wasn't a patch on it, he assured us.

When Goose Fair came round Lawrence wanted me to join a party for a jaunt round the Fair, but mother gave a blank refusal. He sent me a postcard from the café where they had tea at a table in a window overlooking the whole panorama of the Fair, and he managed to convey the full flavour of his palpitating excitement. When he got home he wrote a long account of what they had done, and headed the letter 'The Diary of a Butterfly to a Moth'. I maliciously showed it to mother.

'A butterfly to a moth?' she said. 'What does he mean? Who is the moth? Are you the moth?' Her anger helped to mollify my disappointment.

But we had some wonderful outings. Mrs. Lawrence was an active member of the Women's Co-operative Guild, and sometimes she and a friend would make up a party and hire a brake to take us to Matlock, and it was Lawrence who prevailed upon my parents to let my sister and me accompany them. Best of all, though, were the tramps we had in parties of a dozen or so, all young people. These were genuine explorations of the countryside, and Lawrence was always the originator and the leader. He would walk briskly along with his lithe, light step, tirelessly observant, his eager eyes taking everything in, his pale skin whipped into colour. We had an exhilarating walk to Codnor Castle one bitterly cold day in a Christmas holiday, along the frozen black mud of the towing path by the canal, the icy wind whipping a finer ecstasy into our blood, and imparting a flavour that was more than mortal to the sandwiches and biscuits we munched as we went along. The little, crumbling, ivy-covered ruin that Cromwell had demolished was full of the romance of bygone days. We peopled it in imagination with its former inhabitants — ourselves more splendidly situated.

There was a memorable outing when we took train to Alfreton and walked from there to Wingfield Manor, then on to Crich Stand, and through the woods to Whatstandwell where we hoped to get a train home, but found the station locked up. We were tired and hungry, and beyond our train fare could muster only a few pence amongst us to buy bread and butter at a cottage. But we were supremely happy. Lawrence seemed to have a knowledge of the countryside as he had of flowers; he could tell us something about every place we passed through, as if he had already shared in its life.

It was on one of these walks — we had been to the Hemlock Stone, the curious outcrop of ancient rock that stands alone like a sentinel on the very edge of a big industrial region — that I had a sudden flash of insight which made me see Lawrence in a totally new light. We were walking along anyhow, singly, or in twos and threes. I happened to be alone, admiring the bronze tips of the maple in the hedge. Suddenly I turned and saw Lawrence in the middle of the road, bending over an umbrella. There was something in his attitude that arrested me. His stooping figure had a look of intensity, almost of anguish. For a moment I saw him as a symbolic figure. I was deeply moved and walked back to him.

'What is the matter?' I asked.

'It was Ern's umbrella, and mother will be wild if I take it home broken,' he replied.

We walked on together, but I did not tell him what I had seen. This was perhaps the beginning of our awareness of sympathy for one another.

Christmas was a wonderful time. There were parties at one house or another during the holidays, and always thrilling charades at our house, with Lawrence directing things, and father joining in the play like one of us. Then towards midnight, to escort our friends through the Warren and over the dim field path, singing, with the stars flashing above the silent woods, and the pale light over the water, was perhaps the most wonderful bit of all. We seemed to be living in a world within a world, created out of the energy of the imagination. Life in those days was full to the brim, pressed down, and running over.

Lawrence was loath to admit that boyhood was over. He was most reluctant to begin shaving, and was hurt when people chaffed him about the pale hairs on his chin. My sister criticized him severely. He wasn't decent, she said, going about with such a hairy, untidy face. But shaving was a sign of growing up. Lawrence found the present so good, he wanted it to last.

ADOLESCENTS

My first real step into life outside home came when the local education authority drafted the pupil-teachers of our district to the Ilkeston Pupil-teacher Centre. At first we were housed in the schoolrooms of a Wesleyan chapel, and it was there that Lawrence received instruction both for the King's scholarship and the matriculation examinations. Later on accommodation was found for us in some rooms over the Carnegie library near the church, and whenever I think of those rooms I smell again the strong odour of the new, pale yellow chairs and desks. The two years of my attendance at the pupil-teacher Centre — I was seventeen when I started — stand out for me as the two most completely happy years of my life. It was the acme of childlike completeness before the inevitable break-up out of which maturity, if it ever comes, must proceed.

I knew quite well that the manner of our education was a beggarly makeshift, but for me it was wealth beyond price. We went for only two and a half out of the five school days, having to teach in school on the other days. But to sit down in a class and be taught, no matter how crudely, instead of struggling all day trying to teach children, or sitting alone at a table in the middle of a noisy schoolroom 'studying'; to mix with a number of girls of my own age and occupation; the long early morning walk to the railway station, and the novelty of the short journey by train, these things filled out the days with wonder and delight. And when the mellow chimes of the church clock drifted across the market square to us in our classroom, I could not escape the feeling that in spite of the meanness of our situation, we were the heirs, and in a sense the fellows of the scholars of all time. I laughed at myself for entertaining such far-fetched notions, but they refused to be driven away entirely. I had longed so acutely for education — Lawrence used to say I suffered from what Carlyle called the Englishman's hell, the hell of not getting on. But it was not that. Right from infancy I had been aware of a world that glimmered beyond the surrounding world of fact, and I dreaded lest the circumstances of my life should shut me out, compel me to live, as it were, in the dark, and prevent me from ever becoming a sharer in the feast of the human spirit. And here, in our pupil-teacher Centre, I felt was the beginning of a way.

Lawrence's sister A. and I were in the same class, but being a pupil-teacher in a Board school, A. was no newcomer. I was attached to a poverty-stricken National school, and was looked upon as coming from the backwoods, and I was not in the least surprised that at first A. held aloof from me to see how I shaped. I had known beforehand that this would be her attitude.

So I made no approach to her, and when she saw I was finding my level quite independently she sought me out and we were good chums during our Centre days. We used to travel together, and climb the long hill of Bath Street side by side, A. usually carrying a school-bag bulging with books she would never require. In class we read *The Tempest* together, looking over the same copy. Miranda's noble speeches fired my spirit, and I murmured to A., 'That's just what I believe.' 'Humph, I think it's rubbish,' was her whispered rejoinder.

Occasionally Lawrence attended Centre at the same time, though being our senior he normally went on other days. I remember seeing him sitting apart at a table doing matriculation work. He smiled across at me, and I saw again his uniqueness, how totally different he was from any of the other youths. What this difference consisted in is difficult to put into words, though it was most palpable to the eyes. There was his finely shaped head with small, well-set ears, and his look of concentration, of being more intensely alive. There was his sensitiveness, too, his delicacy of spirit, that, while it contributed vitally to his charm, made him more vulnerable, more susceptible to injury from the crudeness of life. His hair and skin were light and his build delicate. He was proud of his small hands, extremely clever hands they were, equally deft at arranging sweet peas in a vase or at sowing the seed. But there was another quality of lightness about him, something that seemed to shine from within. He and I were beginning to be aware of this difference, and it made a common ground between us. We didn't speak of it, but it was there, a point of attraction.

When we were alone we talked of many things we would never dream of mentioning if anyone else was present. Religion was the first of such topics and I felt surprised when Lawrence began to talk so seriously. Until then I had looked upon him as something of a scatter-brain.

But that was in very early days. Lawrence would only be sixteen when we first talked about religion, and he was clearly perplexed by what passed for religious life amongst us.

'What does it *mean* to them?' he asked slowly, thinking hard. 'Does it mean anything at all? I don't think it means much to me.'

We each regarded our mothers as deeply religious women and in many talks we tried to find out what significance the religion they professed had for them. It was the beginning of Lawrence's groping into experience to find a value that might serve as a guide. There was little analysis of the elements of religion at this stage – that came later – but there was a serious attempt to find a practical value. Lawrence talked a good deal about 'faith' and 'works' and seemed divided in his own mind as to which was the true expression of the religious life. Our respective mothers were the standards of measurement and he finally summed up the argument by saying:

'I suppose your mother's "Mary, Mary" — I'm afraid mine's "Martha, Martha".'

By the time of Centre days Lawrence was beginning to wonder about himself and to realize that he possessed outstanding intellectual gifts. I remember very well a conversation when he and I happened to be on our way home together. It was perhaps the first of many times when we talked about his uniqueness, though of course we never called it that.

'When an individual has more of any quality than other people I think it ought to be shared, don't you?' he asked tentatively. I agreed, and he continued:

'When one has bigger mental gifts, for instance, I think they ought to be used to help other people. That must be what they're given us for, don't you think so?'

After a pause he said slowly, feeling for his words:

'Perhaps I shall be something some day, I mean a bit more than ordinary. If ever I am, I should like to have a big house — you know there are some lovely old houses in the Park with gardens and terraces. Wouldn't it be fine if we could live in one of those houses, mother and all the people we like together? Wouldn't it be fine!'

While he was speaking I had so clearly the knowledge that he must inevitably move far beyond us, and felt that he knew it himself, and was trying to devise some means of not severing himself from us all. His idea did not attract me, nevertheless, and I suggested that we might not agree if we all lived in the same house. He was vexed at my doubt.

'It *would* be all right, I'm sure it would,' he said. 'People aren't really bad, not when you get to know them.'

I remained sceptical, knowing that I could never fit in with such a scheme. But Lawrence cherished the notion, and liked to dwell on it in those days.

When his apprenticeship was over and he drew his first month's salary as an uncertificated teacher Lawrence said that he wanted to buy a toy horse for my small brother, one big enough for him to sit on and be pushed along. It was Hill Top Wakes, and we went together to the Wakes ground, but the glare and smell of the naphtha flares, the raucous music, and the crowd had little attraction for us, and soon we walked away towards Eastwood. At the shop next to the old druggist's we selected the toy horse. I couldn't think of letting Lawrence spend the money required for a big horse, so in the end he bought a fairly small one. He was rather disappointed with his purchase, but knew it was wiser so. Then he suggested that we should have an ice, and we went to the newly-opened confectioner's shop in the main street and ate our ice in the screened-off portion at the back. We had never done anything of the kind before and it had the flavour of adventure. It was a beautiful night and on the way home Lawrence said that instead of turning to go up the hill we would take the longer walk through High Park wood, and we emerged from the comparative gloom of the trees into the soft radiance of moonlight. When we came to Felley Mill where the two brooks ran across the road the whole world seemed drenched in silence and the whiteness of moonlight. It was indescribably beautiful, almost unearthly, and very moving. Lawrence began to talk of love and of his mother with deep feeling.

'A. says she loves her, but she doesn't,' he said. 'She can't, or she'd never treat her as she does at times.'

By this I understood not that A. treated her mother badly, but that her conception of love was of a different nature from Lawrence's. And all the way up the hill Lawrence walked by my side, making me aware in short, almost incoherent sentences how deep, how vital was the feeling he had for his mother. Not to be out-done, I spoke of the sympathy that had always existed between my mother and me, but he would not admit it on the same plane.

'Your mother *doesn't* love you,' he said. 'It's the boys she cares for, not you. Can't you see it? It's only them she loves.'

At the last gate he handed me the brown paper parcel containing the toy, and after lingering a moment, drinking in the beauty of the scene, he turned for home like a man in a trance of love. This happened a week or so before his twentieth birthday.

When our family left the old homestead we had perforce to leave the Congregational chapel on account of the distance. There was no Congregational chapel in the village near us, and somehow we could not make ourselves at home in any of the numerous little Bethels with local preachers, so we went to the church that stood on the hill. It was new, a conscience gift from the land-enclosing aristocracy, and looked modern and utilitarian. Lacking tradition of any kind it had no roots in the place, having been foisted upon the people just as the commons had been filched from them not very many years before. Its atmosphere was chilling. The place was not even dead, for it had never been alive, and was merely of a piece with the leprosy of industrialism. There was never more than a handful of people besides the Sunday school children, to hear the local colliery magnate lisp his way through the morning lessons, and we who had been accustomed to hearing a reasoned discourse delighted to pick holes in the curate's string of platitudes that did duty for a sermon. As time went on I became sensible of the beauty of the Book of Common Prayer, but try as I would I was unutterably depressed by the spiritual coldness of church and the stifling air of patronage. So as we grew up we returned to the chapel at Eastwood, where we had roots and traditions of a sort. My father's interest in chapel activities had waned after the Welsh minister went away, and he attended only when now and again, he drove mother and the little ones down to morning service. Once on the way home he over-took Lawrence, also returning from chapel. Father drew up, 'Jump in, Bert,' he said, and brought Law-rence home for the day, prompted mainly by his desire to discuss the sermon with him.

The chapel at Eastwood became the centre of our social life. There was a Literary Society, and we all paid our shilling for a membership card. I was wildly dis-appointed once when some lecture to which I had looked forward with extravagant anticipation came, and my brother 'didn't feel like turning out'. Mother refused to let me go alone, though the lonely field path had no night terrors for me. I was only appeased when Lawrence, who went to the lecture, told me 'it wasn't up to much'. Another time there was a social, and I called for A. Lawrence thought he wouldn't go, he had his homework to do. A sudden impulse made me look at him and say, 'I wish you would come.' He did not reply but I saw his face change. A. and I set off together, and the first thing I saw on arriving was a group of some four or five youths solemnly fishing in a box with a magnet. I was dismayed, and fervently hoped Lawrence wouldn't come. A few minutes later he walked into the room in that alert, expectant way of his, and I felt too ashamed to speak to him. I had expected the social to be an affair of spontaneous fun and gaiety, and was depressed by the commonplace reality. A ruddy young man with florid tenor voice sang 'The Boys of the Old Brigade' and 'The Old

Shako', and I could have cried when everybody applauded with gusto.

After Sunday evening chapel a little company of family and friends would walk in twos and threes to the Lawrences' house. There was the rustle and scent of Sunday clothes, and that indefinable tightness in the atmosphere that always made me feel slightly sick. A general talk would go on, with Lawrence giving quick conversational change all round. One could feel a tension between him and the other members of the family, as though they were afraid he was going to elude them. Mrs. Lawrence, in her black dress, would sit in the low rocking chair like a little figure of fate, coldly disapproving, while Lawrence fetched cakes and pastries out of the pantry, which he would press upon us who had a long walk home. Sometimes we went into the parlour, and A. would play the piano while we sang 'The heavens are telling', 'O rest in the Lord', 'Yes, the Lord is mindful of His own', and the exquisite 'Hymn to Music' Lawrence liked so much. It was exciting, but there was an undercurrent of hostility running strong beneath it all. I was always glad when we got out on the road again, and Lawrence invariably accompanied us.

By this time the Lawrences had left 'Bleak House' and had moved to a slightly larger one some five minutes' walk away. Lawrence showed me over this house with quiet pride. It had a little entrance hall, with the stairs and the doors to the other rooms opening out from it. There was a cooking range in the scullery as well as in the living-room, a china closet in addition to the pantry, a cupboard under the side window where the school books were kept, and from the big window of the living-room was the view over the roofs of Eastwood to the square church tower standing high above. The garden was pleasant and adjoined a field. This is the house that Lawrence describes in *Aaron's Rod*, where the husband returns surreptitiously at night. It was a comfortable house, comfortably furnished, and Lawrence was justly proud of his home.

Ever since we had become pupil-teachers Lawrence had set himself to help me with my lessons. He used to call himself 'your self-appointed mentor' and often adopted a pedagogical attitude towards me. I on my part was so hungry for any crumbs of knowledge I ignored his occasional hectoring. I returned from some errand on a Saturday afternoon of blazing sunshine to find him sitting on the stone bench at the back of the house in the shade. Directly he saw me he drew a thin algebra text-book out of his pocket, one of his old High School books, and showed me where he had copied out the definitions, postulates, and axioms of Euclid on the inner covers. He said in his excitable way:

'Look here, I've just discovered you have to take maths. in your exam., so you'd better begin.'

Without more ado he began to rush through the definitions with me, always assuming that I had followed his explanations. Even earlier than this he had started giving me French lessons, and as my examination drew near he helped me more systematically. It was arranged that I should call at his home for my French lesson on Friday evenings as I returned from the Centre. Friday was the night when the little market was held in the open space in front of the Sun Inn, and we were often left alone while Mrs. Lawrence went to the market. The father I rarely saw. He was always out in the evenings.

We talked of many things besides French once the door was closed and there arose the magical sense of being alone together. We tried to find out the differences in our own characters. Lawrence told me that I was high and very deep, whereas he was very broad but comparatively shallow.

'It's like this,' he said, taking a piece of chalk from his pocket and drawing spirals on the board below the mantelshelf. 'Your impulse is to go higher and higher, towards perfection, and mine is to go forward, on and on, for aeons and aeons . . .'

'What is an aeon?' I asked.

'Time past all reckoning. Beyond for ever and for ever,' he replied with shining eyes.

It was during the year when he was an uncertificated teacher in the British School at Eastwood that Lawrence first spoke to me about writing. We were in the field that ran alongside the Warren when he said quietly:

'Have you ever thought of writing?'

'Oh yes,' I replied at once, 'I've thought of it all my life. Have you?'

'Yes, I have,' he said in the same quiet tone. 'Well, let's make a start. I'm sure we could do something if we tried. Lots of the things we say, the things you say, would go ever so well into a book.'

This was a new idea to me and seemed to move things forward immensely. But I was preparing for my examination, and he did not press it at the moment. He was evidently trying to find himself. One night when I went for a French lesson he said:

'I knew it was your step outside — like a man's, yet not a man's.' Then looking at me with eyes alight, he said softly:

'It will be *poetry*.'

I took fire at that.

'Well, isn't that the very greatest thing?'

'Ah, *you* say that,' he replied. 'But what will the others say? That I'm a fool. A collier's son a poet!'

'I can't see that that has anything to do with it,' I answered sincerely. 'What does your father's occupation matter?' Lawrence and his father had little connection with one another in my mind. He shook his head, and we went on with the lesson. We were reading Victor Hugo's *Waterloo*, very difficult for me. Lawrence drew a little plan in the book to show the position of the different armies.

'*L'inattendu*,' he said. 'The unexpected. It's the

unexpected that happens,' he continued enigmatically. Soon after eight o'clock we closed our books. Lawrence made up the fire and we put on our outdoor things. He turned the gas low, locked the door, and put the key on the scullery window ledge. I dreaded to hear a foot-step approaching to break the magical quality of our association. When we were alone together we were in a world apart, where feeling and thought were intense, and we seemed to touch a reality that was beyond the ordinary workaday world. But if his mother or sister returned, bringing with them the atmosphere of the market-place, our separate world was temporarily shattered, and was only recaptured with difficulty. So we always tried to set off before anyone returned.

Our way led us by Moorgreen pit and the quiet of the night was punctuated by the metallic rattle of the winding engine and the rhythmic sighing of the ventilating fans. I cannot recall our conversation with exactness. We talked about books and writers, and about life, gropingly, trying to find the hidden reality behind the appearance of things. Towards one another we were utterly unself-conscious except for a strong feeling of mutual sympathy. We were too content with the present to look into the future, and too deeply interested in the enigma of life to think of personal relations. Even then I had the feeling that our walks and talks through the damp, windy autumn evenings were important, and would be memorable. There was something creative about them, a growing and a taking shape of some intangible thing. An ineradicable loyalty to Lawrence grew up in me; his significance seemed beyond that of an ordinary man. I felt that I was in the presence of greatness, and the facts of poverty and obscurity were irrelevant. Once in our talks Shakespeare's name came up:

'That can never be,' said Lawrence. 'Shakespeare was the product of his age. Everything was somehow concentrated in him. Things are so split up now. There can never be another Shakespeare.'

Another time he said to me in great earnestness:

'Every great man — every man who achieves anything, I mean — is founded in some woman. Why shouldn't *you* be the woman I am founded in?'

Our Friday evening lessons were not always undisturbed. Occasionally, one or other of the girls who drifted so casually in and out of the house would come in and sit watching us quizzically, and the atmosphere would become charged with curious cross-currents of feeling. There was one girl in particular who delighted to create this electric atmosphere. She had a ready wit and a caustic tongue, and her gibes flew like arrows. Lawrence would sit with his head lowered over the book, trying to let the storm pass over him, and making short rejoinders only when he was directly appealed to. His mother went about with a subtle smile, half-amused, half-ironic. The mark for all the sly innuendo was of course myself. I was too confused to speak.

59

Besides I didn't dare to open my lips lest I should burst into tears, which was precisely what my tormentor was aiming at.

This particular girl, who could be lavish in her good nature on occasion, seemed to reserve a special venom for any couple who showed signs of falling in love. I heard her tell Lawrence, with every mark of conscious rectitude, how she and a companion would set themselves to annoy a courting couple. They would dog their footsteps, following close on their heels, and destroy any possibility of intimate talk. She pointed out a young man and girl, and said, 'Addy and I did them last Sunday night.'

She seemed to expect Lawrence's approval, but he looked too pained to reply.

The clannishness that was such a marked feature among collier folk did not make Lawrence's position any easier. On the way home I reproached him for not saying one word on my behalf. His reply was brief and emphatic.

'I never take sides,' he said.

When the Christmas term came to an end we discontinued the Friday night lessons, and worked at our house when Lawrence came up, as he usually did, on Saturday afternoon. Sometimes we sat in the little recess in the kitchen while mother was bathing the small children in front of the fire. It used to irritate her beyond bearing to hear us going through Euclid's theorems, for when the French lesson was over

Lawrence always asked if there was anything else I wanted, and I would pass my difficulties in algebra and geometry on to him. This association of work and play inevitably drew us together, and a fine understanding grew up between us. The flow of Lawrence's sympathy set in my direction and awakened a like response in me. We sprang from the same roots, we had grown up together, our vital impulses were in profound sympathy, it was in the nature of things that we should be drawn to one another. We did not speak of love although we knew it lay ahead, something that would have to be faced. But the time was not ripe, and the world that arose spontaneously around us in the moments when we were alone together was such that we wanted to prolong it while we could. In this we doubtless acted unconsciously. There was a feeling of something between us that was rare and precious. A shadow seemed to fall at Christmas when Lawrence said, inviting me to a party at his home:

'I *would* come and meet you, but already they're beginning to say I care more for you than for them. It isn't that,' he continued earnestly, 'they don't understand.'

During the Christmas holidays Lawrence said several times:

'We must read *Coriolanus* together,' and one afternoon he came up with his volume of Shakespeare under his arm and we sat down and read *Coriolanus* straight away. I wondered at his look of puzzled concentration, and felt that the play had a significance for him that I had not grasped.

'You see, it's the mother who counts,' he said, 'the wife hardly at all. The mother is everything to him.'

Lawrence was always tirelessly occupied and spent much of his spare time painting flower studies in oils and in water colours. He would sit on the sofa under the window in the living-room, often singing to himself in an undertone as he worked, quite undisturbed by the work and talk going on around him. He painted a study of fruits for me, figs and dark green leaves, and sent it with a note saying it was a gift of a day of his life. The time between Christmas and Easter when I was working hard for the King's Scholarship examination had a quality of rich intensity. Life seemed preparing to burst into flower. One day in February Lawrence sent a note by my father asking me to meet him at the entrance to High Park wood. The day before he had been with a friend to a wood where snowdrops grew wild and he brought a bunch for me. I fastened the flowers in my coat.

'No, not there,' he said, 'nearer your face,' which I somehow felt to be a rare compliment. As we walked through the wood he talked to me in his rapt way about Blake, telling me what a wonderful man he was, quite poor, who taught himself everything he knew; how he made pictures and wrote poems that were interdependent, and did the printing and engraving himself, in fact producing the book entirely by his own hands. He told me that Blake's wife was a poor girl whom he taught to read, and also to print and engrave, and what a marvellous helpmate she was to him . . . For a little time we lived with Blake and his wife.

When we went in the house, fresh from the crisp air, Lawrence's face eager with talking, my father laughed at us, but my thoughts were with William Blake and his wife. They began to talk about *Jane Eyre* which most of the family happened to be reading just then.

'It was a funny sort of courtship,' father said.

'Yes, it was a courtship without a kiss,' Lawrence replied, at which my father laughed again, and said:

'It was a dry job, then.'

It was about this time that Lawrence exclaimed vexedly:

'Our A. is getting awfully reticent nowadays. She goes out and she won't say where she's been. But as for me I have to tell them every single thing I've done — and said almost.'

My examination was held just before Easter, and left me with a curious empty feeling of having nothing to do. On Good Friday Lawrence came up to sow the flower seeds in our front garden — another task he had taken upon himself. He brought the seeds, sweet peas, shirley poppies, eschscholtzias, and others of his own choosing, and debated seriously whether to sow the sweet peas in a row or in several small circles. My job was to fetch and carry. While we were busy Lawrence said:

'Charles Lamb says that if a childless man would know the joys of fatherhood let him sow seeds and watch them grow. So here are the joys of fatherhood in a penny packet of seeds!' And something in his voice made me see him again, as a man apart.

On Easter Sunday my brother cycled to chapel and I walked down alone. After the service I went with Lawrence to his home. His mother and elder sister E., who was now married, were in the house, and I was aware as always of the undercurrent of hostility. Lawrence was drawing my attention to a volume in the bookcase and E. said in a petulant voice:

'When are you coming to see me, our William?'

'*Jamais*,' replied Lawrence, and glanced at me with a swift smile.

'What do you mean?' she asked suspiciously.

'Oh, I'll come some time,' he answered lightly.

We set out together and had our marvellous walk as far as the field path. At the gate Lawrence leaned towards me and said:

'I shall come up to-morrow — early.'

I went home with a singing in my heart. He would come up to-morrow — early, and what more could heart desire? My brothers were going out cycling, my sister to Liverpool with her fiancé, but I was well content to stay at home when Lawrence was coming up — early.

I spent the morning with mother and the small children, feeling still a little spent after the strain and excitement of the examination days. In the front garden the clumps of narcissi stood in shadowed stillness. I began to expect Lawrence soon after midday, but the afternoon passed, and when at last he wheeled his bicycle through the big yard-gate he was not the Lawrence of the night before.

'You said you were coming early,' I reproached him. He made no answer and avoided my glance. When tea was over he suggested that we should read some French and we went into the stackyard and sat on a log beside the hay-stack. Our dog Trip, a big white bull-terrier, came up to us with doggish delight and lay at our feet. To my surprise Lawrence drove him away:

'Go away, Trip,' he said. 'We don't want you, you're not nice.'

We read a little, but soon Lawrence closed the book and began to speak in a strained voice.

'This . . . this friendship between us . . . is it keeping even . . . is it getting out of balance, do you think?'

My mind barely grasped his words. It was his voice that warned me.

'I think it is keeping in balance,' I replied, bewildered. 'I don't know what you mean.'

'I was afraid,' he went on, as if the words had to be forced out, 'that the balance might be going

65

down on one side. You might, I thought, I don't know, you might be getting to care too much for me.'

I felt my heart turn cold, and replied:

'I don't think so. I haven't thought about it.'

He was silent.

'But why are you saying this?' I asked in deep dismay.

'Well, they were talking last night, mother and E. E. asked mother if we were courting.' He spoke with difficulty. 'They say we either ought to be engaged or else not go about together. It's the penalty of being nineteen and twenty instead of fifteen and sixteen,' he concluded bitterly.

I began to understand.

'Ah — I always thought your mother didn't like me,' I said quietly.

'It isn't that, you mustn't think that; mother has *nothing* against you,' he urged. 'It's for your sake she spoke. She says it isn't fair to you . . . I may be keeping you from getting to like someone else. She says I ought to know how I feel,' he went on painfully. 'I've looked into my heart and I cannot find that I love you as a husband should love his wife. Perhaps I shall, in time. If ever I find I do, I'll tell you. What about you? If you think you love me, tell me, and we'll be engaged. What do you think?'

The world was spinning around me. I was conscious of a fierce pain, of the body as well as of the spirit. I tried not to let him see my tears. As clearly as if in

66

actuality I saw the golden apple of life that had been lying at my finger tips recede irretrievably. We sat some moments in an ashen silence.

When I could speak I told him with truth that I had not thought about love, and that anyhow I couldn't become engaged under such circumstances. He made a movement as though some obstacle was cleared out of the way. A blankness came over me and I had to make an effort to attend to what he was saying in a lifeless voice.

'Very well then, we'll decide what we're to do.'

'There's nothing to decide,' I said. 'We'll have nothing to do with one another.'

'No,' he said with decision, 'we *shall* have something to do with one another. We have so much in common, we can't give it all up. Mother said we needn't give everything up, only we must know what footing we're on, that's all. Life isn't so rich in friendship that we can afford to throw it away. And this is the only friendship that's ripened,' he ended pathetically.

I maintained that there was no footing at all, it would be better to drop everything. But he would not hear of it.

'No, we shall *not*. We shall not give everything up. It means too much to us. We can't give it all up. There's the question of writing, we want to talk about that. And there's the French, we can go on reading together, surely? Only we'll read in the house, or where they can see us. And chapel, that's important.

67

You must keep on coming, and I'll ask Alan not to cycle and then he can walk home with us. And when we go down the fields we'll take the youngsters with us. We needn't let people think we're on a different footing from what we are, that's all. Only we *must* go on talking to one another.'

I listened in silence, stunned and indifferent. He had evidently come up with the plan all worked out. Presently he asked, miserably:

'Will you tell your mother?'

I replied that I should not.

'Shall I tell them, then?' he said.

'No,' I answered, my tears getting the better of me. 'They'd be awfully angry and tell you never to come again.'

He turned and looked at me with wide, distraught eyes, and I said:

'It has nothing to do with them. I manage my own affairs.'

We sat a little while in silence and misery, with the dusk coming on. When we went into the house mother exclaimed:

'Why, Bert, is something the matter? You're so white. You've sat out there and got cold.' Then to me: 'You shouldn't let him sit out like this, you ought to think.'

I made no answer and Lawrence said:

'I'm all right.'

He sat on the sofa, looking painfully white. The

children's painting-box lay open on the table. Lawrence glanced at it, then took a sheet of paper from an exercise book and wrote briefly. He handed the paper to me and I read:

'The children's painting-box needs replenishing. Who will subscribe? I open the list. D.H.L., 1s.'

Soon he said he would go home. Ordinarily I should have gone with him to the barn to fetch his bicycle and open the gate, but I drew the two small children on to my lap. At the window Lawrence turned and gave me an unforgettable look. I clung to the children and we began to sing the humorous ballads they were so fond of. Mother said, 'I'm sure there's something wrong with Bert, he's so white. And why has he gone home so early?'

I was glad that my sister was not sharing my bedroom that night. I could not have endured anyone to know the humiliation I suffered, and the sense of irreparable loss. For I realized that life was completely changed, that there could never be the same sympathy between us again, so deep that it was unconscious. I knew, too, that a cruel injury had been done to young life; the delicate fabric of our relationship had been mutilated deliberately. The issue of love in its crudest sense had been forced upon us while we were still immature and unprepared. I felt that it was a cruel stroke designed to kill what was only in process of formation. In a letter to me five years later Lawrence described it as 'the slaughter of the fœtus in the womb'.

In all that he had said one sentence alone had significance for me — the words, spoken with difficulty, 'I have looked into my heart and I cannot find that I love you as a husband should love his wife.' I was bound to believe him, and that being so nothing else mattered. What we kept and what we rejected was irrelevant, since the central focus of love was null. I was too ignorant and unacquainted with life to understand that Lawrence used the word 'love' in a restricted and special sense. I understood the word only in its total application. Love split into its component elements was something outside my comprehension. And I had no faith in or even desire for a friendship in which love was ruled out in advance. My instinct was to break off completely. Yet I couldn't bring myself to tell my parents; there was nothing I loathed so much as a domestic upheaval.

A couple of days later a note came from Lawrence saying he hoped I was not grieving.

'A man can do so many things,' he wrote. 'He reads, he paints, he can get across his bicycle and go for a ride, but a woman sits at home and thinks.' He added that he would come up on the Friday and read some French with me. When he came we placed our chairs near the back door to be in full view of the household. But I felt humiliated and was unable to keep my mind on the French reading.

He made me promise that I would not be 'stupid', but would go to his home now and again as if nothing had happened. When we went into the fields Lawrence called the two small children to accompany us. They came running in delight, an ecstatic puppy bringing up the rear. Lawrence wanted to talk about poetry, but I felt scornful of a poet who needed a couple of children and a puppy circling around as unconscious chaperones. The talk was not a success; we ended by playing with the children.

When Sunday came my brother again cycled to chapel. As soon as the service was over I went out and took the nearest turn for home. I had not gone far before I heard hurrying footsteps behind me. Lawrence quickly overtook me, but he was not alone; with him was a youth I did not like. He upbraided me bitterly for rushing away. He particularly wanted to show me some roses he had been painting. What with pleading and reproaches he prevailed upon me to turn back and look at the roses. After this my brother walked down to chapel, and the three of us returned together.

Lawrence insisted on my going to tea at his home and meeting his mother. We exchanged a seared glance but never made any reference to what was uppermost in our thoughts.

STUDENT DAYS

LAWRENCE attended the Beauvale Board School as a child, where, he used to tell us, the head master had the unpleasant habit of drawing unfavourable comparisons between him and his brother Ernest. At the age of eleven, however, he won a scholarship tenable at the Nottingham High School. He set no store on knowledge for its own sake, perhaps because he could acquire it so easily, and he told me that it would probably have been better for him if he had never won the scholarship. It was a great strain, he said, when one was only eleven, to have the long walk to the station and a daily train to catch. There was always the anxiety lest one should miss it, and again he was obliged to be away from home for the midday meal. Lawrence considered his scholarship a doubtful blessing.

On leaving school at fifteen Lawrence had for a few months a clerical post with a firm of manufacturers of surgical instruments in Nottingham, but this was interrupted by the attack of pneumonia, and he never returned to the warehouse. About a year later, in the autumn of 1902, when he had enjoyed to the full the freedom of a long convalescence, a vacancy for a pupil teacher occurred in the British School at Eastwood, and the minister of the Congregational chapel, who acted as correspondent between the managers of the school and the local education authority, asked Lawrence's mother if she would let 'Bertie' fill the post. So Lawrence entered upon a two years' apprenticeship. At first his studies were directed by the head master of the school, but in 1903 he was drafted, along with other pupil teachers, to the Ilkeston Pupil-Teacher Centre.

Lawrence's Centre days were very happy. The head master of the Centre quickly perceived his unusual gifts and also, I think, something of his unique personality. Anyhow they got on extremely well together, for Lawrence was a most conscientious and thorough worker. His essays were read out as patterns to the class, and I remember the quiet pride of his smile when he told me. In December, 1904, he sat for the King's Scholarship Examination, and came out in the First Division of the First Class. As his apprenticeship did not end until the following July, our Centre head master volunteered to coach him for the London Matriculation Examination, which he took in the following June. Lawrence felt the strain of examinations severely, and was always sure he had done badly. On the Saturday evening before the examination week we were all in the garden, my parents and the little ones, Lawrence and I. Father happened to be holding a bundle of rhubarb under his arm, and Lawrence, gazing intently at the pink ends of the rhubarb stalks, murmured:

'I'd much rather be describing that rhubarb than sitting for matric.' And during the week he wrote to me of the misery of 'pen-driving in the city heat'.

For the next year Lawrence taught as an uncertificated teacher in the British School at Eastwood, saving most of his earnings towards his college expenses. It was during this year that he began the writing of what eventually became *The White Peacock*. In September, 1906, he entered Nottingham University College as a normal student for a two years' course of training.

Although he had matriculated Lawrence did not wish to take a degree course. His real interest centred on his writing and not on his studies. The professor who was at that time head of the Normal Department, however, persuaded him to take up an Arts degree course, and promised to give him some special tuition in Latin. Lawrence also arranged to have some private lessons from our Scotch minister. This was in the autumn of his first college year. The lessons went on perhaps for a term, and Lawrence informed me, rather savagely, that he had 'broken the back of the Latin', but soon after this he told me that the professor at College was unable to give him the extra help he had promised.

'He can't spare the time for it,' Lawrence said. 'I know he can't pull it in with all he has to do, but why did he promise?' So he dropped the degree course and the lessons with our minister came to an end. He told me this with obvious satisfaction. He was glad to be rid of the bother of working for a degree, and he settled down to his writing and the ordinary college course.

Lawrence entered College in a mood of wistful anticipation. He felt it might be a step into a fuller life; he hoped for a lead of some kind, for contact with things that were vitally alive. In this he was acutely disappointed. He said to me before the course began, 'Surely one should get *something* from those men,' i.e. the tutors. The truth was that he got nothing. He made no essential contact with any member of the staff. The nearest approach to a personal relationship was with a lecturer popularly known as 'Botany' Smith. He apparently did perceive that Lawrence was an unusual individual, for the latter said to me one day with a touch of vexation, 'Botany Smith says I'm not *possessed* with an idea, I'm *obsessed* with it. What do you think, is it true?'

He even got so far as to be invited to tea at Mr. Smith's, but as Lawrence put it, 'Botany's baby developed measles' at the last moment, so he never went to tea.

The only member of the staff he genuinely admired was the head of the Department of Modern Languages. 'He's my favourite Prof.', Lawrence said. And again: 'He really *is* a gentleman. He's quite elegant. He leans back in his chair and points to the blackboard, too elegant to get on his feet. And he addresses us as "gentlemen". He's sarcastic, of course.' But there was never any personal contact. Lawrence merely admired this professor from a distance as a scholar and a gentleman.

His old and now deceased professor of Education Lawrence characterized as a well-meaning but timid and ineffectual man. I used to hear him telling my brother with malicious chuckles how this professor would go to no end of trouble to get the men students together away from the girls in order to talk to them 'as man to man'. Then all he could do was to stand up in front of them looking uncomfortable, making vague allusions, and beating about the bush, never succeeding in coming to his point, whatever it was he wanted to say.

'As man to man,' Lawrence would repeat derisively. 'Why can't he say what he's got to say and have done with it, if he's really got anything to say. He's frightened of the whole business. He no more dare call a spade a spade . . .'

Lawrence was perhaps rather fond of old Principal Symes. At any rate he recommended me to attend a course of Saturday morning lectures on the Metaphysical Poets (who were not metaphysical at all, said Lawrence) given by Principal Symes, only warning me that the lecturer mumbled so, I probably shouldn't be able to make out a word he said.

'But they'll put him in the smallest room, so perhaps it will be all right,' he said. I went to the lectures, and Lawrence was there, too, keen and alert, taking notes. We must have got beyond the Metaphysical Poets

77

because I remember with what feeling the Principal recited to us the lines from Wordsworth's 'The Lost Love', shaking his grey head:

> But she is in her grave, and, oh,
> The difference to me.

Occasionally after the lecture Lawrence would take me to some quiet street where we could talk and ask me intently what I thought of the last pages of writing that he had brought to me. Then he would catch a midday train home, and I, returning at tea time, would be greeted by his quick, bright glance as he sat with our family at tea. For the rest his attitude towards the college staff was one of slightly cynical tolerance. Sometimes on Saturday evening he would mimic one of them for our amusement.

It may be that he never quite got over the treatment meted out to his first essay. The subject, I think, was 'Autumn', and Lawrence began with a reference to Augustine Birrell, saying he would take a flying leap into his subject. He was obviously trying to strike an arresting note. He brought the essay to me after it had passed through the hands of the English Mistress. She had apparently interpreted his attempt to attract attention as impertinence. The essay was heavily scored in red ink with corrections, emendations and exhortations in the best manner of an elderly schoolmistress putting a forward youth in his place. Lawrence had to write it again — 'Give me a *proper* essay this time.' He was mortified at being treated 'like a school-kid.'

'I know it isn't an ordinary essay,' he said; 'it wasn't meant to be, and I thought she'd have the wit to perceive it. But I'll give her the kid's stuff she evidently wants,' he concluded in chagrin. I was surprised to see him so hurt at this reception of his essay — after all, what else could he expect? It would seem that the mistress soon forgot the incident, for Lawrence used to say she was 'quite sweet' with him, but he wrote no more experimental essays for her.

Lawrence never quite lost the impression that the Normal students were regarded as 'school-kids'. He was actually a year or two older than the average student, while in the matter of psychic and emotional development he was of course immensely in advance, and the petty restrictions weighed more heavily on him. There was nothing adult about the life in College, and there was a decided atmosphere of repression, and this was probably at the bottom of his deep disappointment with college life.

'It's different with the engineers,' he used to say. 'You should see the way they go about the place. They look down on us, of course — school teachers!'

An important part of the college training was school-practice, and Lawrence spent some weeks in a school that was regarded as one of the most advanced in the town. In common with nearly all students he detested this part of the training. He told me what extraordinary

essays were produced in the top class, and how proud
the teacher was of them.

'He makes them do it, of course. Full of onomato-
poetic words, just the sounds that animals and birds
make, in an essay on spring — sheer imitation. It's vile,'
said Lawrence, 'absolute ruin of their spontaneous expression. He thinks it's fine, but it's very bad,' he said,
shaking his head with a look of pain.

Even in those days Lawrence used to declare that
the main purpose of education was to teach people how
to use their leisure, or rather how to use themselves.
He denounced vehemently the teaching of subjects
like arithmetic in evening schools.

'What they ought to do,' he said, 'is recreational
work. Teach the adolescents to sing and dance and
do gymnastics, and make things they enjoy making.
It's a crime to expect lads to do sums at night after a
day in the pit.'

The subject he enjoyed most of all in college was
music, which of course was singing. He liked the Folk
songs, particularly the ballad of 'Henry Martin' and
'I sowed the seeds of love'. We bought the song book
in use at College, *A Golden Treasury of Song*, and had
great times singing 'I triumph, I triumph', 'The Lay
of the Imprisoned Huntsman', 'Vulcan's Song' and
practically everything in the book. I have seen Lawrence standing in the open doorway of the cowshed
while my brother was milking, humming a tune from
the sol-fa notes by the light of the hurricane lamp for

the latter to learn. And he once persuaded my brother to cycle the twelve hilly miles into Nottingham to listen to a rehearsal of the College concert. But we often sang without the piano, just sitting round the parlour fire, from the National song-book, sometimes taking two and even three parts, and in all this Lawrence was the moving spirit.

Lawrence advised my father not to send me to College.

'Don't let her go,' he said, 'it isn't worth while. They grind them all through the same mill. They'll make her just like all the others.' So I qualified by taking the external Certificate examination, teaching in school all day and working at home in the evenings, quite independently. Later on, Lawrence told me that if he had known what College was like he would never have made the sacrifice of those two years and all the expense, but would have qualified in the same way that I did.

All the time he was in College Lawrence was working continuously at *The White Peacock* (called 'Nethermere' in those days). He completed it for the first time by the end of the first college year, and during the second year he entirely rewrote it, altering and developing the story a great deal. He was writing poems too, in a small thick note-book with the college arms on the cover. He passed all his writings on to me, secretly, and insisted upon a criticism, or at least, I was to tell him what I thought of them. When he had finished *The*

White Peacock for the second time he said: 'Everything that I am now, all of me, so far, is in that. I think a man puts everything he is into a book — a real book.'

In the final examination of the Board of Education Lawrence had six distinctions: Education, French, Botany, History, Geography, and Mathematics. Ironically, he had no distinction in English. He always said that he passed examinations not by the amount he knew, but by sheer mother-wit.

'It isn't what I know,' he used to declare. 'When I first see the questions I always think I can't answer one of them. It's only when I've looked into myself a bit that I begin to see what to put down. But it's pure mother-wit I do it from, not knowledge.' On one of his birthdays we had given him Motley's *Rise of the Dutch Republic*, and he said he owed his distinction in history entirely to that work.

When I found I was not to go to College I told Lawrence of my ambition to matriculate and eventually work up to a degree. He became rigid at once.

'Why do you want to take matric.?' he asked dictatorially. For the moment I could think of no reason except that I was fond of study and rather enjoyed the excitement of an examination. I said something of this in reply and Lawrence answered severely:

'The reason you want to take matric. is because some rather nice girls you know have taken it. That's no reason why you should. It would be no end of a fag for you, and you might not pass after all, and think what a disappointment that would be, not to mention the expense.'

Then, doubtless aware of my crushed silence, he said in a milder tone:

'You might so easily become a blue-stocking, you know.'

There was an instance of a girl-student in College who was awarded a valuable scholarship in biology. Lawrence spoke passionately against her.

'She's a grub,' he said, 'grubbing for facts like some people go grubbing for money. They might have given it to a man, who would have made use of it.'

When his fit of spleen was over he said:

'It isn't because they've given it to a woman that I object. It's not that at all, really. But she'll just go on piling one bit of knowledge on top of another bit of knowledge, and make no creative use of it. Whereas perhaps a man would.'

The Lawrence that came out of College at the end of two years was a different man from the Lawrence who entered. For one thing he had come up against the materialist attitude to life and religion and it seared his youthful freshness. We were still regular attenders at the Congregational chapel where our minister used to preach interesting sermons that were more lectures than sermons, and on the walk home we would discuss the sermon and religion in general. This was the time when the specific Christian dogmas came up for discussion, particularly after we had read the Rev.

R. J. Campbell's book *The New Theology*. Such things as the Virgin Birth, the Atonement, and the Miracles we talked out and discarded as irrelevant to the real matter of religion. Far more than in any dogma, Lawrence was interested in the question as to how the old religious ideas stood in relation to the scientific discoveries that were sweeping away the familiar landmarks. On one of our walks home he gave my brother and me a vivid description of the nebular theory of the universe, and he was troubled by the discrepancy between such a hypothesis of the origin of things and the God postulated by the Congregational chapel. He resented the tone of authority adopted by the conventionally religious people, including his mother. He said, 'Even mother doesn't like me when I'm different. I've got to be as they are, or else I'm all wrong.' He used to complain that in chapel one had to sit still and seem to agree with all that the minister said. He would have liked to be at liberty to stand up and challenge his statements. It was a matter of grief to him, too, that whoever opposed the orthodox teaching was cast out of the church, which claimed to have a monopoly of the right way of living.

Lawrence had an idea of writing to our minister telling him of the agnostic authors he had read, particularly J. M. Robertson, T. H. Huxley and Haeckel, and asking him to define his position with regard to the standpoint of these writers. The letter was to be signed by the three of us, Lawrence, my brother (who was four years his senior) and myself. I thought it was an excellent method of getting the minister to say where he stood, and warmly supported the idea, but Lawrence drew me up in his sharp way:

'It's all very well for you,' he said, 'you'll get none of the blame. I shall be the young man gone very much wrong.'

Probably the thought of his mother held him back, for the letter was never sent to the minister.

There had been a moment in his early student days when Lawrence had hinted to me that he might enter the ministry. I felt sceptical. I was sure he had it in him to plough a deeper furrow than the ministry offered. I did not feel, either, that he wanted to be a minister. It was doubtless his mother's suggestion. Such a thing would have been dear to her heart. On a Sunday evening when for the moment he and I were alone, he took up a Bible and said with a defiant look:

'If the Bible gives me a clue, then I shall enter the ministry.' He opened the Bible at random but the message was inconclusive. This was before he had read the rationalistic authors who made such an impression upon him.

During his years at the University he completely outgrew the conception of life that chapel and all it stood for offered. It was based too much upon negation. He said:

'The chapel system of morality is all based upon

"Thou shalt not." We want one based upon "Thou shalt".'

It was not the moral rule in particular that Lawrence was up in arms against, but the meagreness of outlook, and the refusal to acknowledge any other attitude to life as being worthy of consideration. The influence of the University as such played very little part in his liberation from religious dogma. It came as a natural growth. He seemed to feel himself compelled to take up a rationalistic standpoint with regard to religion, although it made him miserable. When I said that I was sure of God's existence, he asked me coldly for my proof. . . . Yet at the same period, when my brother was admitted to membership of the chapel and remained for the Communion service, and afterwards made some irreverent remark, I could feel that Lawrence was deeply shocked. He would try to represent himself to me as a complete materialist, but he was too emphatic to be convincing.

Once when his elder brother was on a visit and had been discussing religious beliefs with their mother, Lawrence said to me with a grin:

'Ma's much more upset about G. than about me.'

'Isn't that rather surprising?' I asked.

'Ah, he's older and fixed, that's what she thinks. I'm young, I shall return to the fold,' he said, enigmatically.

It was during these years that Lawrence seemed to lose much of his spontaneous gaiety. In earlier days the whole family, from father downwards, would light up at his coming. But now he often came into the house in a brooding, abstracted mood, and would sit quiet, as if withdrawn into himself. The eclipse of his sunny nature was probably due as much to the growing complexity of his inner problems as to any influence of the wider world. But he was always vividly alive when he began to talk.

Lawrence was not sorry when the college years came to an end, except for the anxiety of getting a job and having to leave home. He had made no significant friendship. He thought teaching very hard work. 'To be able to teach Standard IV properly,' he would say in his vehement fashion, 'you need to know an enormous lot.' And he often said, 'The worst of teaching is, it takes so much out of you and gives you nothing in return. You never know what you've done, or if you've really done anything. Manual work is much more satisfying. You can *see* something for all your pains, you *know* whether you've done the job well or not, but with teaching you *never* know.' At other times he would say he had not enough patience to make a good teacher, and in that one respect he compared himself with Carlyle, whom we were reading at the moment. 'I bet he was an awful teacher,' Lawrence said; 'he'd be impatient and irritable, wouldn't he?' I never took these grumblings too seriously, because I knew what a quick, intuitive sympathy he had with people, particularly children, and I was sure there was a comradely give and take between him and his pupils that, like charity, covered a multitude of sins. He used to say he was lacking in a sense of justice. He wrote to me: 'You are so just. I guess you never punish the wrong kid. As for me, I put up with them until I can stand them no longer, then I land the nearest, and as likely as not, he's innocent.' After he had been teaching for a year in Croydon he said with grim mirth, 'When I first went to Croydon I couldn't teach for nuts.'

It would be a mistake to suppose that Lawrence was definitely unhappy in College. As he often said, it took a good deal to bore him. His capacity for enjoyment was much too strong for College to make him unhappy. All the same he was glad when the course came to an end. It had been a period of disillusion and a progress in isolation. College and all that it implied had been weighed in the balance and found wanting.

As he said to me once in a tone of deep chagrin, 'I've never really had a father.' What he was asking perhaps unconsciously of the University was that it should partly make up for his lack of a father and give him a spiritual and intellectual lead into life itself, and this is hardly deemed to be the job of university professors.

Teaching in Lawrence's day was one of the sweated trades. At the end of his arduous and expensive training he could command in his home county a wage of slightly over thirty shillings a week. He was bitterly

chagrined at the situation and refused to offer his
services to any education authority that would pay him
less than £90 a year. It was not until October, after
being without a post for three months, that he was
appointed assistant master in a Croydon school at a
yearly salary of £95. Lawrence out of work was a sar-
donic figure. He spent much of his time at the farm,
handing his manuscript over to me, and accompanying
my brother about the farm work.

Lawrence's work in the Croydon school was very
different from what it had been in the British School
at Eastwood. He told me that he was responsible for
Art and Nature-Study. Occasionally he asked me to
send him specimens for his nature-study lessons.
Once he asked for twigs of the sallow-willow, and gave
me the most precise directions as to which tree in the
Warren I was to gather them from. When spring came
he wrote with delight about the flowering almonds, and
sent me a box of the blossom because we had never
seen the miracle of the flowering almond in our countryside. I never had the impression that Lawrence was unhappy as a teacher. It was simply that he felt his job
was writing and not teaching, consequently he be-
grudged having to spend the freshest hours of the day
in school when he wanted to be doing the work he was
urged to do from within.

LITERARY FORMATION

DURING the convalescence that followed the attack of pneumonia when he was sixteen Lawrence made a habit of writing long letters to us, sometimes several in a week, which he would send up by my father. They were accounts of what he had been doing or reading, bits of himself put down on paper, often very amusingly, with all the joyous abandon that was such a strong characteristic of his at this time. The letters were addressed sometimes to one, sometimes to another, occasionally to the family as a whole — 'Dear Haggites,' and we all read them and laughed over them, for we looked to Lawrence for most of our entertainment. It was only by imperceptible degrees that his letters came to be addressed chiefly to me, but still, as I thought, intended for the family as a whole. I said to him, 'Of course, I always pass your letters round for everybody to read,' and he replied, 'You needn't pass on *all* my letters for everybody to read.' Thus we two became the correspondents, but father was always the carrier. Now and again he would forget to deliver a letter, and then would exclaim several days later:

'Oh, by Jove! There's a letter from Bert in my pocket,' and I would search through the pockets of his rough tweed coat until I came upon the folded sheets of exercise paper. We never used envelopes in those days.

One of the most treasured possessions of the Lawrence household was a set of large volumes bound in green cloth containing long extracts from famous authors. The books had belonged to Ernest, and were regarded with a reverence amounting to awe. Lawrence must have made many literary acquaintances through the medium of these volumes. As a mark of rare favour I was once allowed to borrow one of them, but the favour was never repeated.

The first book I recollect Lawrence bringing to me was Louisa Alcott's *Little Women*. We thought the story delightful, and set about finding correspondences. I was Jo, there was no doubt about that, and Lawrence was Laurie. 'Only not quite so nice, do you think?' he said with a glance that asked to be contradicted. Not long afterwards he brought Watts-Dunton's *Aylwin*, and then was very contrite because he thought the ghost scene might have frightened me.

'I ought not to have given it to you,' he said repeatedly, and asked anxiously if mother was angry with him.

Both his family and mine were members of the library which was part of the Mechanics' Institute at Eastwood and was open only for two hours on Thursday evenings. How it came about that Lawrence and I usually went to the library together to choose the books

for our respective families, I don't remember, but the
visit to the library was at that time the outstanding
event of the week. As a rule I should put the books to
be returned in the milk-cart, and father would leave
them at his home. Lawrence would change the books
for us, if it happened to be wet and I was unable to
go, and send up the new ones next morning. But I
always went if possible, though Lawrence inevitably
did most of the choosing. He would take possession
of my list and pounce on the book he was looking for;
he always seemed to know just where to look for it.
We were both excited by this hunting among books.
Even then he seemed to be acquainted with nearly
everything in the little library. We had also to bear in
mind the varying tastes of the two families, and the
matter of selection was sometimes a lengthy business.
On more than one occasion when I placed the books
we proposed to take for our family upon the counter,
the old librarian, who gave his time and services to the
Institution, would regard me gravely over his glasses,
and say:

'Young lady, you are entitled to one bound volume
and one magazine,' but he rarely insisted on the letter
of the law. Then Lawrence and I would set off for my
home literally burdened with books. During the walk
we discussed what we had read last, but our discussion
was not exactly criticism, indeed it was not criticism
at all, but a vivid re-creation of the substance of our
reading. Lawrence would ask me in his abrupt way

93

what I thought of such and such a character, and we would compare notes and talk out our differences. The characters interested us most, and there was usually a more or less unconscious identification of them with ourselves, so that our reading became a kind of personal experience. Scott's novels in particular we talked over in this way, and the scenes and events of his stories were more real to us than our actual surroundings. We read Rider Haggard at about the same time, but somehow he never provided the same rich basis for discussion. I remember how Lawrence pressed me to read Anthony Hope's *Rupert of Hentzau* and *The Prisoner of Zenda*. 'You will like them, I'm certain you'll like them,' he assured me, and I did like them, but all the same, I felt they were trivial. A quite different book that he recommended me to read and that impressed me profoundly was Dean Farrer's *Darkness and Dawn*. This period, when Lawrence would be 16–17, was a kind of orgy of reading. I think we were hardly aware of the outside world.

When I called for Lawrence to accompany me to the library, if no one else was in the house, he would take a volume of poetry from the bookcase (Longfellow in the early days) and read to me, always, as it seemed, with one ear cocked for an alien footstep. In this way he read to me most of 'Hiawatha', which I thought long-winded and rather thin, and 'Evangeline', which again Lawrence liked far better than I did. He seemed disappointed when I did not care for the poems he read, so I kept my opinion to myself, for I could never bear to hurt his feelings. He used to look so delicately excited, sitting there on the sofa, his head resting on one of his small, vigorous hands, and the other with fingers ready to turn the page, ready to close the book and swiftly put it away if a step should sound outside in the entry. In time he read Tennyson's 'Morte d'Arthur', which I really did like, and 'Lancelot and Elaine', that struck me as a revolting story. But when he came to 'Maud', dwelling especially on the lyrical passages, and read:

> Birds in the high Hall garden
> When twilight was falling,
> Maud, Maud, Maud, Maud,
> They were crying and calling,

which evoked memories of our own wood, then I thought that was what poetry should be like. Later on he would read 'Ulysses' and would often quote:

> Though much is taken, much abides.

Other poems he read to me time after time were 'The Lotus Eaters' and 'The Lady of Shalott', which he somehow hinted applied to me, and 'Locksley Hall', where again he conveyed the impression that he was telling me something about himself.

Scott was succeeded in our affections by Dickens, with *David Copperfield* pre-eminent. I was aware even then that Lawrence felt an affinity with the hero of that story — 'the nicest young man in the world', he would quote mischievously. *Bleak House* and *Dombey and Son* were great favourites. And to say that we *read* the books gives no adequate idea of what really happened. It was the entering into possession of a new world, a widening and enlargement of life. There was *The Cloister and the Hearth* that we all tried to read together, Lawrence and those of our family who were old enough to read, almost snatching the book out of one another's hands in our eagerness to follow Gerard's thrilling adventures. And how we each described the particular bit of the story that had given us the greatest thrill! Then we read Fennimore Cooper's *Last of the Mohicans* and *The Pathfinder*, with its impression of the expanse of level lake and silence, and R. L. Stevenson's *Treasure Island* and *Kidnapped*. But when Lawrence spoke of *The Master of Ballantrae* there was quite another tone.

'Do read it,' he begged. 'I want to know what you think of it. It's not a bit like Stevenson's other books.' *Lorna Doone* was a story after our own hearts, which we all re-enacted in fancy on our own Annesley Hills. One of the patches of woodland we named Bagworthy Forest, and we scoured down the hillside with imaginary Doones at our heels.

It was on a wintry Sunday afternoon that we explored Felley Mill Farm for the first time — a little crowd of us, my elder brother and sister, my younger brothers, Lawrence and I. Like Annesley Lodge Farm it was unoccupied, the poisoned ground lying fallow, recovering from intensive rabbit farming. We went cautiously through the little side gate into the garden, down which the windows of the two parlours looked blankly. There were snowdrops under the windows, and we gathered some, putting them with ivy leaves which we pulled from the stone wall beside the mill-race, where the wheel used to be, and where now the water slid down with a ceaseless rush into the pond below. The mill-pond was on our left, higher than our heads. We watched the water rushing down and smelt the acrid odour from the mould under the ivy leaves. Then we went through the little gate at the end of the garden and up the steep slope of the sluice, and crossed to the far side of the pond. As there was no one to forbid us we went to the extreme end and walked over the ice to the islet covered with low alders and brushwood. It was pure adventure. The snowdrops and the ivy leaves and the smell of the earth mould, the ceaseless rushing of the water and our own excitement created an impression of something more real and permanent than our actual presence there. We seemed momentarily to have penetrated to the abiding spirit of the place.

With *Adam Bede* and *The Mill on the Floss* we found ourselves in deeper waters. Lawrence adored *The Mill on the Floss*, but always declared that George Eliot had 'gone and spoilt it half way through'. He could not forgive the marriage of the vital Maggie Tulliver to the cripple Philip. He used to say: 'It was wrong, wrong. She should never have made her do it.' When, later on, we came to Schopenhauer's essay on *The Metaphysics of Love*, against the passage: 'The third consideration is the *skeleton*, since it is the foundation of the type of the species. Next to old age and disease, nothing disgusts us so much as a deformed shape; even the most beautiful face cannot make amends for it.' Lawrence wrote in the margin: 'Maggie Tulliver and Philip.' Maggie Tulliver was his favourite heroine. He used to say that the smooth branches of the beech trees (which he especially admired) reminded him of Maggie Tulliver's arms. Over *Romola* he shook his head: 'Poor George Eliot, she said the writing of *Romola* made an old woman of her.'

A book that exercised a real fascination over him was *Jane Eyre*. He seemed to brood over the relationship between Jane and Rochester, whose attitude in particular interested him. 'He calls her a *thing*,' he said to me. 'You know, where he finds Jane in the rose-garden, and he says, "You curious thing." How could one say that in French? It would have to be *chose*. It wouldn't go at all.'

Thackeray's *Vanity Fair* took the household by storm, my father being as eager as any of us. We found a big illustrated volume of *The Four Georges and English Humorists*, and the rollicking Dick Steele and the prim Addison stood out as real figures, the first of the journalists. It was at the house of Lawrence's head master that we came across a volume of Hogarth's drawings and delighted in their bold portrayal of life. There also we found a big volume of Swift's writings, and read a short account of his life. Swift, towering menacingly above his age, impressed us deeply. Lawrence told me about Stella and the *Little Journal*, and we pondered their strange love story.

This might be called the second period of our reading. The first was a sheer revelling in books, the second was almost purely receptive, then we reached the stage which in my mind coincides roughly with my introduction to Palgrave's *Golden Treasury of Songs and Lyrics*, when I was eighteen. This became a kind of Bible to us. Lawrence carried the little red volume in his pocket and read to me on every opportunity, usually out in the fields. He must have read almost every poem to me at one time or another, but those that stand out most clearly in my memory are Shelley's 'The Invitation', 'The Recollection', 'Rarely, rarely comest thou', 'Ode to the west wind', and 'Swiftly walk over the western wave'. Of Wordsworth there was 'The Solitary Reaper', 'I wandered lonely as a cloud', and the 'Ode on Intimations of Immortality', while Keats' 'La Belle Dame Sans Merci' seemed to have the tang of our own dank meadows. These, with others, he would read to me over and over again, and he pointed out that Book IV comprised nearly half the volume.

'Getting nearer to our own day,' he said significantly.

In Book III he was very fond of Cowper's two poems to Mary Unwin. Underneath the second of the two he wrote: 'Poor Cowper, when he felt he was going mad again.' He liked Burns, and when he had read 'Mary Morison', he said, smiling: 'No one was quite so deft as Burns at turning a compliment.' We had many favourites in Book II. Lawrence adored Herbert's 'The Gifts of God' and talked to me about the mystical quality of the poets of that age. Against Shirley's 'Death the Leveller' he wrote in my copy: 'This poem De Quincey says he heard sung in a chamber of a tiny Welsh inn where he was staying awhile during his rambles. The unseen singer was a young Methodist girl, and although used to operatic performances De Quincey was more pleased and delighted with her song than he had ever been before or since.' Lawrence underlined:

> Only the actions of the just
> Smell sweet and blossom in their dust.

He liked 'Fair Helen' very much, and later he taught it to his boys in the Croydon school. He used to say that boys ought to learn love poems at school, as a preparation for love in real life. 'The Great Adventurer' was another favourite: 'Cromwell — in love?' he wrote beneath the poem. Book I was for us mainly Shakespeare's Sonnets, and we marvelled at their perfection and their nearness. All this was spread over a number of years, and meant more to our development than one knows how to put into words. At Christmas we exchanged tiny gift books. Lawrence gave me once a selection of Shelley and at other times *The Blessed Damozel* and the *Rubáiyát of Omar Khayyám*, and I gave him Blake's *Songs of Innocence* and *Songs of Experience*.

We read essays, too, at this time. Bacon's *Essays* was one of our set books. Lawrence detested Bacon's calculated moralizing, but he adored Lamb, and dwelt affectionately on 'Dream Children' and 'The South Sea House', and we chuckled over 'A Dissertation on Roast Pig'. He read and liked Emerson's *Essays* and became wildly enthusiastic over Thoreau's *Walden*, especially the essay on 'The Ponds'. I remember Lawrence waiting one morning of a holiday to accompany my brother who was going to work in the Greasley fields, and telling us meanwhile how Thoreau built himself a hut in the woods and lived beside the pond. It was a still, sunless morning, with a brooding light over the landscape, and the atmosphere he conveyed in his description seemed to tally perfectly with that particular morning.

Then we came to Carlyle. Lawrence said that he was reading the *French Revolution* with Carlyle on one knee and the dictionary on the other. He was loud in his denunciation of Carlyle's affectation of a German style, but he insisted on my reading the book. The stabbing of Marat by Charlotte Corday excited him —

just like a bit out of *A Tale of Two Cities*, he said. We read also *Heroes and Hero Worship* and *Sartor Resartus*. This was in the spring of 1906 just before Lawrence went to College, and his early flamboyant delight in reading was changing into a seriousness that was at times almost frightening in its intensity. He said to me weightily, 'I feel I have something to say,' and again, 'I think it will be didactic.'

Other books that belong to this period were Mrs. Gaskell's *Cranford*, and I remember the glow of his tender delight in that simple tale. And there was *Alice in Wonderland* that we bought for the little ones and revelled in ourselves. A book that Lawrence absolutely forbade me to read was *Wuthering Heights*.

'*You* mustn't read it,' he said in his excited way. And when I asked why not, he said:

'You mustn't, that's all. It might upset you.' I said I meant to read it anyhow, and then he became serious and made me promise I wouldn't. His mother had read it, and I remember hearing her say with comic exaggeration what she would like to do to 'that Heathcliffe', only she pronounced it 'Hethcliffe'.

Once when we had just left his home Lawrence said to me, 'I don't believe they were like us when they were young, do you? Our parents, I mean. I don't imagine mother ever read Carlyle. It was Annie Swan, I think.'

And another time he said:

'I'm sure they don't feel things as we do, I don't care what they say. They talk about them too much.

If you really feel a thing deeply you can't talk about it, can you?'

Lawrence now began to talk definitely of writing. He said he thought he should try a novel, and wanted me to try to write one too, so that we could compare notes.

'The usual plan is to take two couples and develop their relationships,' he said. 'Most of George Eliot's are on that plan. Anyhow, I don't want a plot, I should be bored with it. I shall try two couples for a start.'

It was in the Whitsuntide holiday that he brought the first pages to me. I had been away from home, and returned to find Lawrence waiting uneasily. Out in the fields he gave me the manuscript and asked me if I had any to show him. I shook my head.

'We've broken the ice,' he said in a tense voice. He told me to put the writing away and read it when he had gone. I was to tell him what I thought of it the next time he came. I was interested to find that his story was laid around Felley Mill Farm. These first pages described himself standing on the banks of the mill-pond, watching the fish glide in and out. The farm had a tenant now, and Lawrence had accompanied me there several times on some errand or other. From now on he brought some pages almost every time he came up. He would pass them to me in secret and wait restlessly until we were out in the fields and he could begin to talk about his writing. One evening we were looking for the little purple orchids that were to be found only in the Long Close, and Lawrence was saying:

'I'm afraid it will be a mosaic. My time's so broken up. In the morning when I should love to sit down to it I have to go to school. And when you've done the day's teaching all your brightness has gone. By the time I get back to the writing I'm another man. I don't see how there can be any continuity about it. It will have to be a mosaic, a mosaic of moods.'

What fascinated me about his writing was the way he would weave incidents from our daily life into it. Mother was looking in the wood for the nest of a hen that was laying away, and came across an old kettle containing a nest and a bright-eyed robin sitting on her eggs. We showed it to Lawrence, who seemed moved at the sight. Soon after it appeared in his writing, described with amazing exactness and intensity of observation. Then there was the lark's nest, a mere hole where a cow's hoof had sunk into the soft ground, and the four speckled eggs lying there, so unprotected. Lawrence knelt beside it, almost trembling with excitement. We went to look at it each time he came until at last the quivering bubs lay on the ground, with feathers fine like hairs.

A fragment of conversation about writing and writers comes back to me. We were in the wood where the stiff clay soil was waterlogged in all except the driest seasons, and we were picking our way carefully over the muddy patches.

'You see, it was really George Eliot who started it all,' Lawrence was saying in the deliberate way he had of speaking when he was trying to work something out in his own mind. 'And how wild they all were with her for doing it. It was she who started putting all the action inside. Before, you know, with Fielding and the others, it had been outside. Now I wonder which is right?'

I always found myself most interested in what people thought and experienced within themselves, so I ventured the opinion that George Eliot had been right.

'I wonder if she was,' Lawrence replied thoughtfully. 'You know I can't help thinking there ought to be a bit of both.'

We now began to read the great French authors. We had already done simple tales, *Picciola*, *Jettatura* and *Un Philosophe sous les toits*, and we had read Pierre Loti's *Pêcheur d'Islande* on the cliffs overlooking the blue water of Robin Hood's Bay. Lawrence had a great admiration for French literature and for Balzac in particular. Yet I remember his remarking on more than one occasion that great as the French language was, it had no equivalent word for *wonder* — a serious lack in his opinion.

'I think *wonder* is one of the finest words in our language,' he said, 'and yet the French have no word for it. You'd have to say *merveille* or *étonnement* — not the same at all. And *home* — *chez moi*; it's cold and impersonal compared with the English *home*.' All the same, he liked to imagine that he had a French ancestor. He surprised us one Saturday evening by saying in the tone of mortification that we usually heard when he spoke of his father:

'The latest from father. He tells us now that his grandfather was a Frenchman and fought in the battle of Waterloo, and that his sword used to hang in the shop when father was a lad. This is the first we've heard of it.'

We laughed, and asked Lawrence how, if his great-grandfather was a Frenchman, he came to live at Old Brinsley. Lawrence shrugged his shoulders:

'Refugee, I suppose,' he said briefly.

It was in quite another mood that, standing by the wall at the end of the reservoir and looking along the water, he said sombrely:

'If English people don't like what I write, and I think it's probable they won't, I shall settle in France and write for the French.'

There were times when he was full of doubt and dissatisfaction with himself and everything around him. It was difficult then to see in the introspective young man of twenty-two the youth we had first known, brimming with delight in life and all it had to offer. He used to call these gloomy fits his 'Hamlet' moments.

He was very impressed by Balzac's *La Peau de Chagrin*. He described the story to us minutely, dwelling upon the progressive shrinking of the skin, which involved the diminishing of its owner's life. 'With every wish that was granted, the skin shrank,' he said, demonstrating with his palm. The symbolic implication seemed to oppress him. I was only nineteen when he bought Maupassant's *Tales* for me to read in a translation, telling me to take care my mother didn't see them. They made me wretched. Maupassant's presentation of life seemed to me brutal and one-sided, but Lawrence said I mustn't mind about that. It was the technique that mattered. I could see that he was thrilled to the marrow. Then a few days later came a note full of remorse: 'What am I doing to you? You used to be so vigorous, so full of interest in all sorts of things. Don't take too much notice of me. You mustn't allow yourself to be hurt by Maupassant or by me.' After this came Flaubert's *Madame Bovary*, which Lawrence admired immensely and got very excited about. He also read *Salammbô*, which he said was rather boring. There was doubtless much that I never heard of. We went on with our lighter reading and delighted in *Lettres de mon Moulin*. He read Ruskin at this period, and passed on *Sesame and Lilies* to my eldest brother. During one of the summer vacations when they spent some days together thatching haystacks in the fields at Greasley Lawrence told me he had been reading Virgil's *Georgics* to him, translating from the Latin. This was while *The White Peacock* was taking shape in his mind.

Sometimes we had a play-reading at home. We read *Macbeth* with father taking the part of Macduff, and horrified at the speech he had to make when he came face to face with Macbeth. He stopped to exclaim, 'Oh dear, oh dear! How awful!' Lawrence stood knitting his brows, half-amused, half-vexed at the interruption. He was excited and inclined to be domineering over the play-readings, but we knew him too well to take offence. He admired Ibsen tremendously, and recommended my brother to give me a volume of his plays on my birthday, so we read *Rosmersholme*, which was Lawrence's favourite, and *The Lady from the Sea*, of which he gave us a full description in advance, saying it was the most poetical of Ibsen's plays that he had read. Finally we read *Hedda Gabler* which he thoroughly disliked. I remember how severely he took me to task for omitting a phrase about someone who used to 'keep mistresses'. I simply couldn't read it aloud. Lawrence said nothing at the time, but he taxed me with it later. 'Why did you miss that passage — about mistresses? You should have read it as it stood. What do you want to make such evasions for . . .'

We went to the theatre occasionally. I saw *Hamlet* for the first time with Lawrence and my brother. Lawrence was intensely excited. He went through Hamlet's soliloquy afterwards in our kitchen — 'To be, or not to be . . .' And it was the same when we had seen *Macbeth* — 'Is this a dagger I see before me, the handle towards my hand . . . ?' grasping at an imaginary dagger. It was his characteristic blending of the serious with the comic. Of course we laughed at him, but the two aspects were plainly visible. Going to the theatre was the same as reading, Lawrence identified himself with the play, and for the time being lived in its atmosphere. Now and again we saw a D'Oyley Carte opera — Lawrence was often humming a tune from *Il Trovatore* — and we heard *Tannhäuser*. Once on a Saturday afternoon we went to a Gilbert and Sullivan opera, and on another occasion we saw Galsworthy's *Strife*.

While Lawrence was at college Sarah Bernhardt came to our theatre at Nottingham, and he went to see her in *La Dame aux Camelias*. The next day he wrote to me that the play had so upset him that at the end he rushed from his place and found himself battering at the doors until an attendant came and let him out. He ran to the station to find the last train gone, and had to walk home. He added, 'I feel frightened. I realize that I, too, might become enslaved to a woman.' On the Saturday afternoon he came up and told us all about the play, and showed us how Sarah Bernhardt died in the last scene. He looked quite worn out with emotion.

Lawrence greatly admired George Borrow. He spent a whole sunny Saturday evening up on the Annesley Hills telling me about Borrow's life and about

Lavengro, making the story so vivid that Borrow seemed to be an actual acquaintance. He said that Borrow had mingled autobiography and fiction so inextricably in *Lavengro* that the most astute critics could not be sure where the one ended and the other began. From his subtle smile I felt he was wondering whether he might not do something in the same fashion himself.

We read Meredith, in poetry as well as prose — *Love in the Valley* had a special significance for him. There was Gissing, whose *Private Papers of Henry Ryecroft* he brought to us in a paper-covered edition, and my parents enjoyed it so much. Hardy's name had been familiar in our house since childhood days. Mark Rutherford's *Autobiography* and *Clara Hopgood* Lawrence admired with reservations. He told me that if I ever did write (and he was always urging me to) my writing would somewhat resemble Mark Rutherford's. We read Oscar Wilde's *Ballad of Reading Gaol* and *Intentions*. Lawrence read *The Picture of Dorian Grey*, and earnestly begged me not to read it. He brought some of Aubrey Beardsley's drawings for us to see, and the Irish plays of J. M. Synge. He was enthusiastic about a Nature magazine that came out in fortnightly parts. He came up with the first part one Sunday afternoon and stood by the field gate looking with intense appreciation at the frontispiece, a photograph of a sedge-warbler feeding a young cuckoo. Lawrence's intimacy with nature was a constant revelation. We

spent some of the most exquisite moments of our lives
gathering flowers, ladysmocks and cowslips. Lawrence
pointed out to me that Shakespeare must have noticed
the difference between the thrum-eyed and the pin-
eyed flowers. He said once, 'It's a funny thing. You
love the wood and all this far more than I do, yet I can
describe it and you can't.'

It was during his second year in College that Lawrence
began to read philosophy. I cannot be sure whether he
read Kant at this period, but he advised one of my
brothers to give me Schopenhauer's *Essays* for my
birthday, and read *The Metaphysics of Love* aloud to us.
He translated the Latin quotations in pencil in the
margin. This essay made a deep impression upon him.
He was vehemently of Schopenhauer's opinion that a
white skin is not natural to man, and had a fierce argument with my brother who disputed the statement that
'fair hair and blue eyes are a deviation from type'.
Lawrence said pointedly:
'For me, a brown skin is the only beautiful one.'
He followed the reasoning closely, as always applying
it to himself, and his own case. When he read: 'Accord-
ingly, everyone in the first place will infinitely prefer
and ardently desire those who are most beautiful,' he
broke off to remark:
'That's just the trouble, though. I see what is most
beautiful, and I *don't* desire it.' Schopenhauer seemed
to fit in with his mood. He thought he found there an

explanation of his own divided attitude and he remained under the influence of this line of reasoning for some time. Another book that absorbed him was *The Memoirs of Benvenuto Cellini*. He admitted that Cellini was a scamp, but an interesting one. Renan's *Life of Jesus* belongs to this period, but we were disappointed in it. 'It is Jesus according to the likeness of Ernest Renan,' said Lawrence. The materialist philosophy came in full blast with T. H. Huxley's *Man's Place in Nature*, Darwin's *Origin of Species*, and Haeckel's *Riddle of the Universe*. This rationalistic teaching impressed Lawrence deeply. He came upon it at a time of spiritual fog, when the lights of orthodox religion and morality were proving wholly inadequate, perplexed as he was by his own personal dilemma. My feeling was that he tried to fill up a spiritual vacuum by swallowing materialism at a gulp. But it did not carry him far. He would tell me with vehemence that nature is red in tooth and claw, with the implication that 'nature' included human nature. Yet when he heard the cry of a rabbit tracked by a weasel he would shiver in pain. His dominant feeling seemed to be a sense of hopelessness.

There was Locke's *On Human Understanding*, and Bishop Berkeley who said that everything exists in one's own consciousness. Lawrence used to insist with particular emphasis — 'If God does not exist in my consciousness, then for me God does not exist.' And he carried the argument over to many other aspects of his life at that time. In all his reading he seemed to be groping for something that he could lay hold of as a guiding principle in his own life. There was never the least touch of the academic or the scholastic in his approach. What he read was to be applied here and now; he seemed to consider all his philosophical reading from the angle of his own personal need. He read also Herbert Spencer and John Stuart Mill and William James, whose *Pragmatism* especially appealed to him. He liked also *Some Varieties of Religious Experience* and recommended me to read it.

During his second autumn in College, Lawrence devised a plan for raising a little money. A local journal offered a prize of three guineas for the best Christmas story. Lawrence wrote three short stories, and suggested that I, a college friend, and he, should each submit one story to this journal. As luck would have it the story I sent was accepted and came out under my name. It was a sentimental little story called *A Prelude to a Happy Christmas*, and was Lawrence's first appearance in print. A cheque for three guineas came, so I signed and my father cashed Lawrence's first cheque. As he gave the money to him, father remarked:

'Well Bert, it's the first, but I hope it won't be the last.'

The story that Lawrence submitted himself and that was rejected, he re-wrote, and it subsequently appeared in the *English Review* under the title of *A Fragment of Stained Glass*. The third story probably formed the basis for *The White Stocking*. It was an idealized picture of his mother as a young girl going to a ball at the Castle and drawing out a long white stocking in mistake for a pocket handkerchief.

As my twenty-first birthday approached Lawrence talked to me earnestly about my future — did I want to go into the town or remain in the country? It all depended upon whether I was going to attempt to write. 'If you feel you have it in you to write something as fresh as the dew on the hills,' he said, 'stay in the country and we'll give you books to help you to continue growing. But if you are not going to write, then go into the town and enlarge your experience in actual contact with people . . .' In the end he brought me his own copy of Tolstoy's *Anna Karénina*. He said it was the greatest novel in the world, and we revelled in it, father, my brother, and I. We felt most sympathy in those days with Levin and Kitty, and followed their experiments in farming with deep interest. The book was like a piece of new experience, and the people real individuals whom we could discuss and argue about as though they had been personal friends. Lawrence, however, was more interested in the problem of Anna.

We continued to read poetry. One day in a Christmas holiday Lawrence and I and the girl who had sent the story about the white stocking to the local newspaper, trudged over the frozen snow to the ruins of

Beauvale Abbey. It was a day of brilliant sunshine, and the three of us perched in a tree that leaned over a pond, while Lawrence read Coleridge's *Christabel*. It was upon this ruined abbey that he had centred his story *A Fragment of Stained Glass*. Browning was a great favourite. Lawrence read *Paracelsus* and *The Ring and the Book*. But best of all he liked some of the shorter pieces from a pocket volume of *Selections*, and read to me many times 'Andrea del Sarto', 'One Word More', 'Porphyria's Lover', 'Any Wife to Any Husband', 'Never the Time and the Place', and 'Rabbi Ben Ezra'. These poems he read to me over and over again, usually on a Saturday evening after supper, when my brothers were out, mother and the little ones in bed, and father in his corner engrossed in the *Daily News*.

Lawrence was constantly bringing his writing to me, and I always had to tell him what I thought of it. He would ask whether the characters had developed, and whether the conversation was natural, if it was what people really would say. He found conversation easy and wondered if it was too easy. He feared he had a tendency towards verbosity; perhaps he ought to condense his writing more . . . Saturday evening was the best time for talking over his work, but in a busy household like ours I naturally had to help. Sometimes when he very much wanted to talk, Lawrence would follow me from the kitchen into the parlour and back again from parlour to kitchen until I was free to sit down and talk to him. He always declared that he did the writing for me.

'Every bit I do is for you,' he said. 'Whenever I've done a fresh bit I think to myself: "What will she say to this?" ' And of his poetry he said, 'All my poetry belongs to you.'

I had not a high opinion of the first version of *The White Peacock*, in which George married Letty. Lawrence persuaded me on a Saturday morning when I happened to be going into Nottingham, to take a tram ride out to Basford and bring him word what the registry office looked like. It was a solid, square building, the most unromantic place imaginable. I can see now his bright, subtle smile when I told him my impressions. The next pages of writing he brought to me described George and Letty being married there. The novel, apart from its setting, seemed to me story-bookish and unreal. The upright young farmer, hope-lessly in love with the superior young lady (very con-scious of her social superiority) who had been served shabbily by a still more socially superior young man, married her after a puritanical exposition of the cir-cumstances by her mother, and a highly dubious conjugal life began in the melancholy farmhouse, with, one imagined, Letty always in the parlour and George in the kitchen. Yet in spite of its sentimentality, a thread of genuine romance ran through the story; something in the atmosphere was alive. The poem *Love on the Farm* is a sort of epitome of this early version of the novel, although I knew it originally as two separate poems. I think Lawrence despised the story from the bottom of his heart, for he immediately started to rewrite it. He must have shown it to his mother because when we were on holiday at Robin Hood's Bay I asked her what she thought of it, and she replied, in a pained voice:

'To think that *my* son should have written such a story,' referring presumably to Letty's situation.

In the second writing the story was radically altered and the characters became more like flesh and blood, except Cyril, who remained as he began, old-maidish. Lawrence concentrated upon George, and the figure of Annable emerged, at first only cynically brutal, but later developing into symbolic stature. I was horrified at Annable's first appearance and remonstrated with Lawrence, but he shook his head decisively, and said:

'He *has* to be there. Don't you see why? He makes a sort of balance. Otherwise it's too much one thing, too much *me*,' and grinned.

The only thing I did see, and that obscurely enough, was that Annable seemed to be a focus for all Lawrence's despair over the materialist view of life he felt compelled to accept for lack of an alternative.

Lawrence's extraordinary obsession with game-keepers is difficult to account for. The only encounter with a gamekeeper that occurred during the years of my acquaintance with him took place when he was a youth of seventeen. A party of us, including my three brothers and Lawrence's sister, penetrated unwittingly into a private portion of the Annesley woods. There we found a spot that looked like fairyland — a stream flowing between smooth green banks starred with primroses, which are rare in our woods. We were enchanted; we gathered the flowers and sang and made plenty of noise. Suddenly a burly, red-haired keeper with a youth close on his heels burst through the trees. He took my eldest brother and Lawrence aside and made them give their names. Then he told us all that these 'pimroses' were private property and made us leave our bunches on the ground. We trooped home crestfallen, Lawrence white-faced and still.

The scene in the old churchyard followed almost immediately upon an evening some five years later, when Lawrence and I had walked as far as the disused and crumbling church. We climbed the fence into the churchyard and ventured forward step by step until we could look down upon the terrace in front of the Hall. The next time Lawrence came up he brought the scene of the peacock and the angel, and Annable's caustic comments.

Lawrence entirely rewrote the novel and gave it its final shape during his first year in Croydon, and the story developed into a subtle study in self-portraiture. Cyril and Letty are each aspects of Lawrence, with Emily as a foil to both. George developed from the simple, God-fearing yeoman into the man whose inner growth has been arrested, with the consequent proliferation into decay. It was an immense stride forward from the first conception, and he struck me as a figure of sinister prophecy. It seems to me not without significance that in this first novel Lawrence should portray no fewer than three men whose lives come to complete frustration, while Cyril is a purely negative figure.

The rounding-off of the story Lawrence wrote during our brief moment of harmony. He said in a letter: 'Do you mind if, *in the novel*, I make Emily marry Tom?' I didn't mind in the least. I thought the final turn to Emily's fortunes one of the happiest human touches in the book. Lawrence often said, 'To write, I *must* be happy. I can't get on with things when I'm unhappy,' and I know it was abundantly true.

When Lawrence left home and went to teach in Croydon he found a new wealth of reading in the public library there. Sometimes when he had particularly enjoyed a book he would send it to me with urgent instructions to leave off whatever I might happen to be doing and read it immediately. In this manner he sent me Charles Doughty's *Adam Cast Forth*, and I was especially to note where Eve, after long separation, finds Adam, and he tells her to bind herself to him with the vine strands, lest they be separated again by the Wind of God. Another time, in swift enthusiasm, he sent me Francis Thompson's essay on Shelley; and again there came *Atalanta in Calydon*, and my attention was directed to the lyrics of the choruses.

One holiday, I think it was Whitsuntide, he brought up in great enthusiasm Samuel Butler's *Erewhon*, and out in the fields he told me about the wonderful opening chapter.

'It begins like a book of travel,' he said. 'You'd never dream it was satire. It's so fresh, so romantic, such a sense of a new country. And then he just turns all our ideas of society upside down, but with the greatest seriousness . . .' So he told me practically the whole content of the book as we walked to the Warren to see what new things had come into flower since last he was there.

On an evening of a holiday in the spring of 1909 he read his essay 'Art and the Individual' to a little gathering of the Eastwood intelligentsia at the house of a friend, where he sprawled at full length on the hearthrug, shy at reading his own work. It was a member of this little circle, a Socialist and a Suffragette, who first showed us A. R. Orage's *New Age* which Lawrence took regularly for a time. He liked it far more for its literature than its politics. He was never really interested in politics, and was quickly irritated and bored by the subject. We used to enjoy particularly the *Literary Causerie* by Jacob Tonson.

It was in the library at Croydon that Lawrence found Nietzsche. He never mentioned him directly to me, nor suggested that I should read him, but I began to hear about the 'Will to Power', and perceived that he had come upon something new and engrossing . . .

He wrote to me at one time, 'I read nothing serious now, only Pushkin, very polished and elegant, and the delicate irony of Anatole France's *Isle des Pinguins*'. He read, of course, all the modern English authors. I remember his telling me how Wells' *Tono-Bungay* made him feel in despair about himself.

'Most authors write out of their own personality,' he said. 'Wells does, of course. But I'm not sure that I've got a big enough personality to write out of.'

He liked Galsworthy's *A Country House* very much, and Bennett's *The Old Wives' Tale*, and Conrad's *Lord Jim*. He admired George Moore and sent me *Evelyn Innes* and *Esther Waters*. When he read Olive Schreiner's *The Story of an African Farm* he wrote to me: 'It will wring your woman's heart some day,' which meant that his heart had been wrung by the story. Gilbert Murray's translations from Euripides were a great delight. He gave me *The Trojan Women*, which I think was his favourite, and he passed on to me *Medea*, *Elektra*, *The Bacchae*, and Aristophanes' *Frogs*. He liked Turgenev immensely, and gave me his copy of *Fathers and Sons*, and impressed upon me that I must read *Rudin*. He read Maxim Gorky, but didn't care much for him. He talked to me about George Sand and Alfred de Musset, both of whom he read, and at this time the two great poetic lights in his firmament were Verlaine and Baudelaire. When he sent me a book he would occasionally copy out a verse, or even a whole poem, from one or other of these poets on the fly-leaf.

He was a diligent searcher of the second-hand book-stalls and barrows in Surrey Street, Croydon. There he found a school edition of Wordsworth's poems, which he sent to me, he said, for the sake of *The Solitary Reaper*. On the fly-leaf he copied from *Les Fleurs du Mal*:

Soyez béni, mon Dieu, qui donnez la souffrance
Comme un divin remède à nos impuretés
Et comme la meilleure et la plus pure essence
Qui prépare les forts aux saintes voluptés!

He came across *The Playboy of the Western World* in a tattered condition, had it bound, and sent it to me. On the fly-leaf of this he copied in its entirety Baudelaire's *Sonnet d'Automne*. Another time he picked up W. H. Hudson's *South American Sketches* for twopence and passed it on as a wonderful find, and at various times he sent me a volume of *Don Quixote*, promising to try and find the companion volume, one of Burns' *Letters*, and Sterne's *Sentimental Journey*, drawing my attention to the beautiful type and the fine old leather bindings.

Whitman's *Leaves of Grass* was one of his great books. He would sometimes write, 'I'm sending you a Whitmanesque poem,' when he was enclosing one of his own. There was Maeterlinck's *Pelleas and Melisande* and *The Sightless* that impressed him briefly. At the Christmas that immediately followed his mother's death he sent me Leon Daudet's *Le partage de l'enfant*, saying it would help me to realize the position of the child in a home where the parents do not get on well together. Somewhere about this time Lawrence read Dostoevsky's *Crime and Punishment*, and I remember how he frowned in a puzzled way and said:

'It's very great, but I don't like it. I don't quite understand it. I must read it again.'

The last of all the books that Lawrence passed on to me was *Toil of Men* by Izrael Querido. It was a story of the Dutch bulb farms, told with a brutality that struck me as exaggeration for the sake of effect. I returned it to Lawrence along with several other books shortly before he went abroad in 1912.

This account of Lawrence's reading makes no claim to be exhaustive. It is merely an attempt to indicate the nature and scope of his reading as far as possible in the order in which it occurred. He certainly read much more than is indicated here; he seemed to read everything. His vitality and interest were the same in the sphere of books as in other departments of life. He took in eagerly all that came to his hand, shaping it according to his need, and sharing his zest with characteristic generosity.

CONFLICT

AFTER Lawrence had defined his attitude towards me things went on outwardly as before, but inwardly everything was changed. We had become self-conscious and aware of a barrier. He developed a highly critical tone. If I stooped to touch a flower he would lecture me severely.

'Why must you *touch* in order to enjoy? I can see how beautiful the daffodil is, but I don't want to touch it. What you need to cultivate is detachment. You want to be able to stand aloof and enjoy a thing without any desire to touch it.'

And if I caught up my little brother and hugged him I had fallen into the same error. I must cultivate detachment; that was the great thing, to be detached. I found it very confusing.

On an evening of that same spring (when Lawrence was in his twenty-first year) his sister cycled up to the farm. She had come to tell me something that shocked us all very much. A friend of theirs was in deep disgrace — in A.'s conventional phrase he had 'got a girl into trouble'. On the following evening Lawrence came himself, looking white and upset. As soon as we

were alone he asked me if I had heard about his friend
— they had been High School boys together. He
seemed relieved that I knew. He said his mother
had told him about it that morning. He was very
distressed. His mother had said how terrible might be
the consequences of only five minutes' self-forgetful-
ness. And it seemed to add to the tragedy that the
young people had only seen one another on Sunday
evenings after chapel — so Lawrence said. He
told me these things in a voice that sounded sick with
misery, and I felt very concerned, wondering why he
should take it so to heart. Then he startled me by
bursting out vehemently:

'Thank God . . . I've been saved from that . . .
so far.'

I was puzzled, feeling in the dark about the whole
business, and very sorry for Lawrence's distress. He
seemed relieved after he had told me about it.

In the August before he entered College the
Lawrences made up a party (including myself) and
spent a fortnight at Mablethorpe on the Lincolnshire
coast. This was the first of our seaside holidays, and
Lawrence was full of delightful anticipations — we
would take sketching books and do all sorts of jolly
things. We stayed at a cottage about a mile out of the
little town. A dyke ran beside the road, and we had to
cross a plank bridge to reach the cottage, standing alone
in its garden. Lawrence went over the house in delight.

'It's so comfortable, as nice as home,' he said. There was a mirror over the sideboard and one over the mantelpiece.

'What a lot of mirrors,' he said. 'We shall all get vain.'

'Or else modest,' I suggested. He gave me a quick look.

'Ah, perhaps modest,' he agreed.

It was windy on Sunday morning, and I tied my hat on with a broad silk scarf. Lawrence was looking at me with shining eyes.

'Does it suit me?' I asked, laughing. He turned to his mother. 'Look at her, mother. She says, does it suit her?'

His mother gave me a bitter glance, and turned away, and the light died out of Lawrence's face.

In the evening he and I wandered along the beach waiting to see the moon rise over the sea. We set off light-heartedly enough, but gradually some dark power seemed to take possession of Lawrence, and when the final beauty of the moonrise broke upon us, something seemed to explode inside him. I cannot remember now what he said, but his words were wild, and he appeared to be in great distress of mind, and possibly also of body. In some way I was to blame. He upbraided me bitterly, and when I protested he blamed himself, and poured himself out in a torrent of passionate words.

This scene was repeated with increasing intensity on two successive occasions when I spent my annual holiday with the Lawrences and their friends. The second time was at Robin Hood's Bay, when the combined beauty of moonlight and sea, together with whatever effect my presence had upon him, seemed to make him distraught. He talked and behaved so wildly that it is difficult to recall what he did actually say or do. I only remember that he stalked some distance from me like a strange, wild creature, and kept up a stream of upbraiding, or something that sounded like it. When we were climbing the steep little street and I stopped a moment to rest, a swift change of mood came over him. He fell to bitter imprecation of himself, declaring that it was all his fault and he was hurting me. I was aware of a deep tenderness within, that he held in check with an iron will.

On the third occasion at Flamborough the tension was much more severe. Lawrence skipped from one white boulder to another in the vast amphitheatre of the bay until I could have doubted whether he was indeed a human being. I was really frightened then — not physically, but deep in my soul. He created an atmosphere not of death, which after all is part of mortality, but of an utter negation of life, as though he had become dehumanized. And always, somehow or other, it was my fault, or partly my fault. They were unforgettable experiences. I never spoke about them, for I was at a loss to describe them.

At Mablethorpe our favourite way to the sea was a grassy lane between the dykes we called the Green

Way. It led across the single track railway and right into the sandhills. Later on we came across a painting in Nottingham Castle showing just such a bit of the Lincolnshire coast, the yellow dunes and the pale sea-holly. We felt sure it was our own Green Way.

Lawrence's father was with us and one morning he and we young people set off for a long walk over the level lanes. We went to Theddlethorpe All Saints and Theddlethorpe St. Helens and called at a tiny ale-house kept by one Susannah Stones, licensed for six days only. We had bread and cheese and ginger beer, and Mr. Lawrence had a can of ale. We came to a windmill actually at work, and watching the great sails revolve, thought of Gerard in *The Cloister and the Hearth*. On the way home we found watercress growing in a brook, and Lawrence and his father gleefully gathered some to take home for tea. Words cannot convey Lawrence's brimming delight in all these simple things.

I could only afford to stay one week and as Lawrence's father was also going home we travelled together. Mr. Lawrence seemed almost old and inarticulate. All through the journey he sat gazing at the landscape with eyes that perhaps saw nothing, so dim and expressionless was their look. Once he glanced at me; I thought he was going to speak, but he changed his mind and went on staring dimly through the window. Looking back over my week's holiday with its poignant memories of happiness and pain I was not far from tears, and perhaps my companion was aware of it. When we reached our destination he turned in a kindly way to help me with my bag.

The inner change in our attitude to one another grew gradually more pronounced. Lawrence said wistfully:

'If only you'd been a man, things might have been perfect'; then added immediately: 'but it wouldn't have been any good, because then you wouldn't have cared about me.'

He declared I was like Emily Brontë, which I resented, feeling it was a false short-cut to understanding me, like sticking a label on. To all my protests he merely shook his head.

'You *are* like her, you are intense and introspective like she was.'

From time to time I was aware of a clumsy probing into my personality.

'It isn't as if you had a strong intellect,' he said meditatively. Since Lawrence was my criterion in the matter of intellect I agreed cheerfully.

'I don't suppose I have. I never thought so.'

'No,' he said as if in regret. 'No, you're purely emotional.'

'Well, what if I am?' I asked.

'Well, you see, it means that you're governed entirely by your feelings. You don't *think*, you *feel*. There's a lot of difference, you know.'

'Perhaps that's because I am more sure of my feelings than my thoughts,' I replied.

'Yes, but don't you see, that proves you're not intellectual,' he answered. 'Now, as for me, I trust entirely to the intellect.'

I was not sure enough of my ground to challenge him. The painful probing continued. He startled me by saying, reflectively:

'You're not really popular, are you?'

I laughed and said that probably I was not, but anyhow, what did it matter? I was rather hurt when he went on:

'Very few people *like* you, do they?'

'I don't know *very* many people,' I replied.

'That doesn't matter,' he returned. 'The point is you don't get on very well with people.' He seemed to be following a pre-conceived train of thought.

'I get on well enough,' I replied, in vexation. 'Why should I wish to be popular? People like me as well as I want them to.'

'That's just it,' he declared. 'At the bottom you don't really care whether people like you or not.'

'Why should I care? I can't help it, either way.'

'No, but you see,' he said with sudden gentleness, 'there must be some fault in you if *nobody* likes you. The others can't *all* be wrong.'

'But they *do* like me, those who know me properly,' I protested, knowing how hopeless it was to expect the people he had in mind to like me.

Finally he told me I had no sense of humour, and it occurred to me that if it were so I should be too angry to listen to him.

'It seemed at one time as if I had a little, Bert,' I said, half in fun, but he replied crushingly:

'You have absolutely none. Everything has a fixed value for you.'

I hated the process of internal dismemberment and said to him one day:

'What comes next when you've finished taking me to pieces? Will you be able to put me together again?'

He looked startled.

'I *don't* take you to pieces. Only you're so hard to understand.'

This was one side of our friendship. There were still times of intuitive understanding when we were hardly conscious of ourselves as separate individuals. It was only when Lawrence deliberately set himself to apprehend me by way of the intellect that we were hopelessly at odds. I could only reveal myself to him by what I was, and his crude gropings into the recesses of my personality confused me and made me shut up tight. He said once wistfully:

'You'd be easier to understand, you know, if you would be a bit naughty sometimes.'

I knew what he meant and felt guilty, but of something deeper than naughtiness. The invisible barrier that had been raised between us seemed to be freezing the springs of my spontaneity; and the necessity to repress my vital feelings made me cramped and negative. But I could see no way of escape. His attempts to understand me intellectually were paralysing, and the denial of love took all the meaning out of life. I would often wake with a start just before dawn when the air was filled with the unearthly twitterings of the birds, and, realizing instantly the blight that had settled on my life, feel like a castaway on some inhuman shore.

Lawrence often seemed very unhappy. His eyes had a look of suffering. I could feel at times the bitter struggle he had with himself to maintain his position of aloofness. Once a word of endearment escaped him, but he drew himself up and repudiated it with vehemence. He began to tell me that his feeling for me was entirely intellectual and spiritual, and had nothing to do with the physical side of life.

'It comes to this, you know,' he said. 'You have no sexual attraction at all, none whatever.'

I had only the vaguest conception of his meaning, and thought he was telling me that I was unattractive in a general way. I did not feel greatly perturbed, and said:

'Well, how can I help it? Is it my fault?'

'I don't suppose so. It simply is the fact. You are absolutely lacking in sexual attraction, and that's the truth of the matter.'

He told me this at the time when Schopenhauer's *Metaphysics of Love* exercised such a fascination over him. He seemed to find confirmation for his attitude in the passage: 'Because the kernel of passionate love turns on the anticipation of the child to be born and its nature, it is quite possible for friendship, without any admixture of sexual love, to exist between two young, good-looking people of different sex if there is perfect fitness of temperament and intellectual capacity,' which he marked and wrote in the margin '*Qu'en pensez-vous?*'

Maupassant's *Tales* also influenced him in the direction of regarding love as something purely physical. It depressed me greatly.

Lawrence was still a great favourite with our family and visited the farm as frequently as ever. He said sometimes, whimsically:

'Ah, you Haggites see the best of me!' The only one who was critical of him was my elder sister. She saw more of Lawrence at Eastwood than the rest of us, and his tendency to be all things to all people made her feel that he was insincere. When his twenty-first birthday approached we decided to give him a present from the family as a whole. He said he would like pictures to copy. So on a Saturday afternoon Lawrence, my brother and I went to Nottingham, and in an old-established bookshop we found an incomplete series of English water-colours which they said we could have for a guinea. (These are the pictures to which Lawrence refers in his article 'Making Pictures'.) He thought it was far too much for us to spend on him, but accepted them on condition that they were to be regarded as belonging to both families. We had tea in a café near Victoria station, with Lawrence looking radiantly happy. Later he had his photograph taken and sent a copy to us, with a note for me saying that 'the troublesome original would probably come up and bother me the next day'.

At Christmas he gave me a tiny selection of Shelley's poems, for the sake of *The Sensitive Plant*, he said. It was a gift-book and on the inner cover was printed: 'To give it my loving friend to keep.' For some reason Lawrence inscribed it to 'La Curieuse' and told me with scorn in his voice:

'They wouldn't believe me when I said it simply meant "the curious one". They actually had to look it up in the dictionary.'

Our French reading still went on in a desultory fashion, and Lawrence suggested we should each keep a diary in French. He insisted on my keeping one, but I never saw his. I was to put down my *thoughts* (he was emphatic about that) and he would correct and reply in French. He used to ask for my diary each week with a pedagogical air. Once in reply to some entry of mine he wrote '*Pour faire croître quelque-chose, il faut le supprimer.*' That I understood and knew that he was speaking for both of us, but I was puzzled when, another time, he wrote across the page: '*Quant à moi, je suis grand animal.*' I demurred, but he insisted, nodding emphatically, 'Yes, yes, I *am*.'

The question of our relationship was a subject he could not let alone. He would argue the matter from all sorts of standpoints. Once he said suddenly:

'I don't believe in the idea of one man one woman, do you? I mean there isn't just one woman and one only that a man can marry. There might be half a dozen that would do equally well. What do you think? You're not the complement of me, you don't *complement* me in any way. Do you think you do?'

It sounded like something he had been turning over in his mind, probably discussing with his mother, and he wanted to convince himself.

Another time he said with great seriousness:

'The trouble is, you see, I'm not one man, but two.'

I refused to accept the idea, but he persisted gravely:

'It's true, it *is* so. I am two men inside one skin.'

Then he began to tell me that one of his selves could and did love me, but to the other self I had no significance at all. I repudiated the notion vigorously.

'I can't see it,' I said. 'To me you are a whole man. If I am to love you at all, it must be as a complete whole.'

'But I am *not* a complete whole. I tell you, I am two men. One man in me loves you, but the other never can love you.'

There was the deadlock. I could not acknowledge his dual nature, and he continued to assert it. He was continually trying to find some basis for a relationship between us other than the natural one of love and marriage.

'One part of my nature needs you deeply,' he would explain with moving earnestness. 'For some things I cannot do without you. But the other side of me wants someone else, someone different.'

Such a foundation for friendship was totally unacceptable to me because I was convinced that so far as I was concerned love was a whole, a synthesis of all that I was. I could not move from my standpoint, even if I had wanted to. It was the fundamental me, and there was no altering it. Lawrence was equally convinced of his duality, and of the two distinct kinds of 'love'. The argument went on with much expenditure of emotion on both sides, over a period of years. He asked me once if I was acutely aware of him sometimes, and added:

'Because at times I am most acutely aware of you, and I wondered if you were aware of me at the same time. It might be telepathy, you know.'

He would return to the question of our relationship to one another at all sorts of odd moments, as if it were never really out of his mind. During our second seaside holiday at Robin Hood's Bay, a member of the party was reading a novel called *Where the Apple Reddens*, and Lawrence, pointing to the book lying on the sitting-room table, said to me significantly:

'*You* might say that.'

And the following year at Flamborough, when we

were climbing the rocky path from Brunswick Bay, a little in advance of the others, he suddenly exclaimed: 'There are men who would worship the ground you walk on', and I was almost in tears, protesting I didn't want to be worshipped.

Lawrence's father was with us during the Robin Hood's Bay holiday; with us, but not of us, for he found his pleasures apart. I cannot recall what the occasion was, but Lawrence broke into a storm of abuse against his father (who was not present) and then flung from the room. His mother bent her head with a strange smile.

'He hates his father,' she said. 'I know why he hates his father. It happened before he was born. One night he put me out of the house . . . He's bound to hate his father.'

Mrs. Lawrence occupied a remarkable position in her family. She ruled by a sort of divine right of motherhood, the priestess rather than the mother. Her prestige was unchallenged; it would have seemed like sacrilege to question her authority. I wondered often what was the secret of her power, and came to the conclusion that it lay in her unassailable belief in her own rightness.

The search for some basis for a relationship went on like an undercurrent to all our activities. On my twenty-first birthday Lawrence sent me a long letter in the course of which he said:

'When I look at you, what I see is not the kissable and embraceable part of you, although it is so fine to look at, with the silken toss of hair curling over your ears. What I see is the deep spirit within. That I love and can go on loving all my life . . . Look, you are a nun, I give you what I would give a holy nun. So you must let me marry a woman I can kiss and embrace and make the mother of my children.'

Then he added with prophetic insight, 'The anguish that impinges so cruelly upon you now comes only from your association with me. Once you have passed out of my orbit life holds nothing but sunshine for you, of that I am convinced.'

This letter seemed to strike at my very roots, certain though I was of its fundamental untruth. I had no desire to be a nun. My instinct was to achieve some measure of understanding of life, not to evade it. Neither could I believe in his division of love into the spiritual and the physical. It seemed to me entirely mistaken. For divided in this manner 'physical love' became an insult, and 'spiritual love' an abstraction. I felt that each was equally unreal. But from this time he proceeded to develop the idea of the two kinds of love as separate and distinct. He began to tell me that he could marry a girl of our acquaintance from a purely physical standpoint. (This is the girl to whom he refers in the Note to the *Collected Poems* as 'the other woman, the woman of *Kisses in the Train* and *Hands of the Betrothed*'. For the sake of convenience I will call her X.) The idea of such a marriage was sheer blasphemy upon all my notions of human association, but I recognized vaguely that his extreme materialism was nothing but the measure of his spiritual frustration. He tried to reason it out with me.

'Now I could marry X. from the purely animal side.'

'It's a horrible thing to do,' I replied.

'Why is it horrible? Most men marry in the animal way — at least, nearly all men of intellect do. You've only to look round to see.'

'It's insulting to her, to split yourself in two, and offer her half like that.'

'It isn't insulting to her. She'd have the children. Besides, she'd never know.'

'Oh, wouldn't she?'

He made it clear that the 'other half' of himself belonged to me.

'I give you all the best of myself. You don't really want the other,' he pleaded. I was bewildered.

'But I don't understand,' I said. 'If you are going to marry X., what do you want to keep on with me for?'

'Because I cannot do without you,' he replied with intensity. 'The writing, all that side of me, belongs to you. Without you I can't go on.'

'Well, I don't see how we're going to do it,' I answered.

'Why not?' he demanded.

'Because, if you marry someone else, what is between you and me will be bound to come to an end,' I tried haltingly to explain.

'Why must it come to an end?' he asked in fury.

It seemed self-evident to me. I could not imagine how two separate and distinct relationships, both vital, could exist simultaneously. Lawrence appeared to think they could, and insisted with equal force that he and I must never marry and also that we must never part. My position was difficult. I was reluctant to give him the idea that simply because we might never marry I wanted to refuse the co-operation that he said was essential to his work, but I knew with absolute certainty that when he married our co-operation must inevitably come to an end. The argument went on intermittently for several years.

'It's like this,' he said, 'some strands of your nature are knitted with some strands of mine, and we *cannot* be parted.'

Again he would say:

'I can't *make* myself love you, can I? I can't plant a little love-tree in my heart.'

'Of course not,' I replied. 'But then why do you trouble about me? Why don't you leave me alone?'

His answer came with shattering sincerity:

'Because you are necessary to me.'

Sometimes he would say in a sort of desperation:

'It might be disastrous if we were to marry.' And once, pathetically:

'I *don't* want to make a hash of things.'

Another time he said in deep earnestness:

'Some part of me will *always* want you. Some parts

of one's nature are always changing, but another part never changes, and that part will always want you.'

In his aggressive moods he pursued the idea of marrying X. — as an animal pure and simple, he said. But I could never believe that he would be able to do it. He was too vehement; I felt that he was trying to force himself in that direction. Once when we three were together he said to her cynically:

'When one can't attain to genuine love one has to make shift with the spurious.'

X. tittered and agreed, never suspecting its personal application.

On a day in the summer of 1907 Lawrence went to her home to tea, giving me to understand that he meant to find out whether his feeling towards X. was what he thought it was. Some days later he handed me, with a significant glance, the poem *Snapdragon*, in which the lines:

> And there in the dark I did discover
> Things I was out to find:

is a literal description of the situation. But although he had apparently satisfied himself as to the nature of his feeling, he took no action of any kind, but remained as suspended as before.

Finally I said to him:

'Very well, marry X. if you want to, or anyone you like. But when you are married we can have nothing to do with one another.'

This distressed him deeply.

'But it would be *inhuman* not to let us meet some-times and talk,' he said. I wondered if anything could be more inhuman than the situation that already existed.

'Do you think X. would let us? Would any wife?' I asked him.

'But it takes nothing from her. She has the . . . the other side,' he pleaded.

'When you are married you belong to your wife,' I told him. 'Besides, I shouldn't want.'

The deadlock thus complete he would turn his face to the dark fields and exclaim with the vehemence of despair, '*Nothing* matters.'

I could see no way out and thought it would be best to leave home. I told mother I should like to get a post away and she made no objection until she saw me filling in a form of application. Then she said she could not bear the thought of my going away. She began to cry and begged me to stay at home.

'It's on account of Bert that you want to go away,' she said. I acknowledged that it was, and she replied accusingly:

'You would leave *me* because of him.'

My parents never wished that Lawrence and I should marry. As they put it: 'Bert belongs to his mother. She'll never give him up.' They appeared to accept the situation unquestioningly. I told Lawrence of my attempt to leave home. He listened moodily, then said, 'It's perhaps as well for you to stay. I shall be going myself soon.'

We still had our times of wonderful sympathy and understanding, when we left the future to take care of itself. There was an afternoon when we walked out to the Misk Hills, blackberrying, in a glow of happiness. I remember we decided that destiny lay within one's own nature, like the bud inside the plant. Lawrence told me, too, that I could never be entirely romantic, although there was so much of the romantic in my make-up. There was a residue of realism in me, he said, that would always come out. The worst of a romantic nature was that it turned bitter if it failed to develop; and true to his custom of providing concrete examples to prove his theories, he mentioned someone we both knew very well as an instance of a romantic nature turned bitter. Our talks were vital to our development. In them we seemed to become free of a richer, intenser life. Lawrence often said he could talk better to me than to anyone, and sometimes when I reminded him of something he had said, he would exclaim:

'Did I really say that? I didn't think I had ever said anything so fine.'

He was constantly telling me I ought to write; above all, he said, I ought to write lyrics.

'You've read all the best literature, and the finest poetry in the world. You've read hardly any rubbish. You ought to write,' he said.

'It's true, I've scarcely read any rubbish,' I replied.

'It *is* true. And yet you produce nothing,' he said severely.

'How can I write? I've had no proper education . . .'
I objected.

'You've had a very good education,' he retorted.
'You've had *me*. I've been a better education to you
than any academic sort.'

'You've taught me almost everything I know. It
has been wonderful,' I acknowledged. But I was unable to write. I could not detach myself sufficiently
from the strange impasse of our relationship to look
objectively at the world around me. I could only
apprehend things from within, and I seemed to live in
a sort of subjective trance, watching things develop.

Lawrence had found a new name for me. I was no
longer Emily Brontë; I was a pre-Raphaelite woman.
I disliked the new label even more than the old one.
It made me feel that for him I was becoming less and
less of a suffering, struggling human being, and more
and more of a mental concept, a pure abstraction.

One holiday afternoon a party of us, including two
of my brothers and Lawrence's sister, had a picnic on
the Misk Hills. The weather was perfect, and we had
one of those magical times when the very air seemed
to radiate joy. Lawrence returned home with us and
when he and I were alone he began:

'We've had a gorgeous time, but I wonder, are we
wise to have these times together? Won't they make
the ultimate parting harder? I hope you realize how
things are.'

This time I was not only hurt, but offended. I felt,

too, that he derived a perverse pleasure from the theme. I said little at the time, but when he had gone I wrote to him, telling him that he could set his mind at rest. He had explained that he could not love me, and I took him at his word, and would never, never expect him to, so would he please refrain from spoiling the memory of a beautiful day by dragging out this miserable story. I was sick and tired of the whole thing. . . .

I saw him some days later at the close of the College concert. My brother and I had been to the concert, and the three of us came home together. All the way up the hill from the station Lawrence kept asking:

> 'Why did you burn your waxen man,
>   Sister Helen?'

For some time I made no answer, hoping he would stop. But he went on repeating, in a significant voice:

> 'Why did you burn your waxen man,
>   Sister Helen?
> The time was long but the time drew on,
>   Sister Helen.'

At last in desperation I said: 'It was time to burn him.' And he replied, shuddering:

> 'Oh, Mother, Mary Mother,
>   What hope between hell and heaven?'

He had read Rossetti's poem to me, but I disliked its spirit of revenge. For hate and revenge lay definitely outside my orbit; I had nothing to do with them.

That I should hate Lawrence was inconceivable, for I recognized his tragic predicament. It was visible to me in his outward form, in an unfledged look about him, something incomplete. His dilemma was real, not self-imposed, and the only helpful thing I could give him was a sympathetic hearing. I said to him once:

'Let it be as you like, then.' And he took me up passionately.

'As I *like*? Do you think I do as I *like*? If I did as I liked . . .'

Whatever my own lot, it was easier to bear than his, for at least I had the positive value of love, and I was not frustrated as he was by inner division. For myself I had no fear, but there were moments when I saw Lawrence poised dizzily on the edge of an abyss, and I was powerless to help him. There were moments, too, in our desperate struggle, when we seemed to touch another sphere of existence, and it flashed upon me that never here in this life, but somewhere beyond the human bourne lay the unity we were striving for. He perhaps at times felt something similar, because he once exclaimed:

'You push me beyond the very bounds of human consciousness.'

One evening when Lawrence went to fetch his bicycle from the barn he told me that the brake was out of order and that he steadied himself by holding his foot on the front wheel. I begged him to be careful, and when he came again he said:

'It was a good thing you told me to take care. There was a horse and cart nearly at the bottom of Hunt's Hill. . . .'

'Why, did your remember?' I asked in surprise.

'Yes, I said to myself "She told me to be careful," so I braked with my foot. If I hadn't I should have bashed into the cart.'

'Why don't you get it mended? How much would it cost?'

'Half a crown. But I've no money,' he replied.

In my next letter I enclosed a postal order for half a crown, and asked him to get the brake mended. He sent a letter of incoherent protest, but he promised to get it done.

When his College course was over and the long vacation began he brought so much of his writing to me that I had to set my studies aside for the time being. But his work was of paramount interest. He said several times:

'I never shall be able to repay you.'

That seemed to imply a kind of bargain, to me an intolerable idea, and I always replied that there was nothing to repay.

'You don't owe me anything. You give me as much as I give you.'

'That *is* true, it *is* a mutual exchange, isn't it?' he said.

Another evening, in the parlour where so much of our talking and study was done, he said slowly:

'You, more than anyone I know, are capable of living a full life.'

My heart burned, for I knew his words were true, but my opportunities were meagre, save through him.

When he had to leave us to take up his post in Croydon he looked like a man under sentence of exile. I saw his mother.

'What shall *I* do when he's gone?' she moaned. Then she burst out in a sudden odd fierceness.

'And where would he have been without me to call him up in a morning, and have his porridge and everything ready for him? He'd never have got off to College every day if I hadn't seen to things.'

It struck me as incongruous that his mother should make much of these homely services. But I do not think she saw him, or even wanted to see him, as a man of genius. It would remove him too far from her. What she saw was the loving and dutiful son she could claim and keep, and share the day to day joys and sorrows with. They were in close communion, swiftly responsive to one another. 'The Little Woman,' Lawrence used to call her playfully. She knew that he had outstanding abilities and was inordinately proud of him. His going away would leave her days empty and colourless.

He came to say good-bye to us. He was pale and his eyes looked dark with pain.

'Well, Bert, you're going to leave us then,' father said, and much feeling lay behind the casual words.

'It looks like it,' Lawrence replied in the same way.

He set off for home soon after supper. I walked with him to the last gate, where we stopped. He leaned towards me.

'*La dernière fois*,' he said, inclining his head towards the farm and the wood. I burst into tears, and he put his arms round me. He kissed me and stroked my cheek, murmuring:

'I'm so sorry, so sorry, so sorry.'

His words scalded me. I drew away and dried my tears.

'I'm so sorry for this,' he said again in a deadened voice. 'But it can't be helped, it can't be helped.'

'Never mind,' I said, 'it doesn't matter.'

We stood for some minutes seeing the familiar outlines of the landscape in the dim October evening. It was all utterly hopeless, there was no use beginning the old argument again. Presently he said:

'Mother and A. are having a few people to tea tomorrow. Come as well, if you like.'

'I'll see,' I answered; and he got on his bicycle and rode away. I understood the nature of his invitation. It meant, 'Come if you can bear to', for it was now impossible to ignore the fixed hostility towards me. As he had said long ago, he never took sides, at least he never took my side. I tried hard to stay away, but as the time approached some power stronger than my own will compelled me to go. So I filled a small basket with the rosiest of our apples and made that my excuse. It was not a gay party, Lawrence looked white and wretched. I came home early, in deep humiliation. I knew my malady, but years were to pass before I found it adequately described:

> His folly hath not fellow
>   Beneath the blue of day
> That gives to man or woman
>   His heart and soul away.

On his second day in Croydon Lawrence sent me a letter that gave me a shock. It was like a howl of terror. People were kind, he said, but everything was strange, and how could he live away from us all? He dreaded morning and school with the anguish of a sick girl. Finally he said he felt afraid for himself; cut off from us all he would grow into something black and ugly, like some loathsome bird . . . In a postscript he told me not to say anything of this to his mother, he had written to her that everything was all right and he was getting on well. I burned his letter immediately lest anyone should see it. I had known that it hurt him to leave us, but I came nowhere near to guessing how much.

The phase of acute homesickness soon wore off. He settled down to the third writing of *The White Peacock*, and began to explore London, and to write about the lights that flowered when darkness came. At Christmas he came home for a fortnight's holiday, and told us how tiny were the rooms of the house he lived in. But he liked the people. They were homely Lancashire people with two children, one a baby only a few months old. He told us that sometimes only he could get her to sleep at night, by singing his favourite ballad of *Henry Martin*. I remarked to his mother how fond he was of the baby, and she replied austerely:

'Yes, I was glad when I knew there was a baby. It will keep him pure.'

We had no uproarious charades that Christmas, the spirit was lacking. One evening of the holiday Lawrence and my mother were talking about the historic landmarks of Nottingham, and Lawrence, glancing at me, said we would make up a party some day and discover what remained of old Nottingham.

He wrote to me almost every week from Croydon, about himself and his writing and school, just as he had been in the habit of talking. In one letter he said:

'You — the anvil on which I have hammered myself out. . . .'

Only twice in all our long association did Lawrence speak to me directly of sex, and each time he asked me if I minded. During a holiday walk he suddenly said:

'Do you *mind* if I talk to you about sex?'

'I don't think so,' I replied.

'Because Chesterton says that the man who talks about sex to a woman is a brute. Do you agree with him?'

'Why surely, it's the other way about,' I said. 'The man who can't speak properly to a woman about sex is the brute.'

'That's what I think,' he replied. Then he went on

to tell me that some men, commercial travellers probably, had been talking in the train.

'If you had heard them, you'd have had to rush
away,' he said. He never told me what it was he had
heard, but it seemed to have bruised his consciousness,
and he wanted to tell me about it for the sake of relief.

On the second occasion he began by saying:

'We are agreed that Chesterton is the brute, and
I can talk to you about sex.' But I cannot recall with
any clearness what he said further. As far as I can
recollect he seemed to be claiming for himself the right
to know all about the 'worldly' attitude to sex, while I
should remain in comparative ignorance.

'I *must* know about those things,' he said, 'but why
should you want to?'

'I don't want to. They don't interest me,' I told him.

I could not help feeling that the whole question of
sex had for him the fascination of horror, and also that
in his repudiation of any possibility of a sex relation
between us he felt that he paid me a deep and
subtle compliment. I was sure there was something
fundamentally false in this attitude, because of my
inescapable conviction that one must accept life as a
whole.

The old argument went on. There was a sunny
afternoon on the Annesley Hills when Lawrence tried
his utmost to persuade me that love and marriage could
have no part in my life. I made a passionate protest.

'This life here is all we know,' I said, 'like a spell of

daylight between two eternities. How can I ever live completely if I shut out one half of life?'

There were contradictory elements too, and times when he would say:

'Things will come right in the end. I am always hoping things will come all right.'

Then the theme of a 'physical' marriage with X. would crop up again. I have a clear recollection of Lawrence coming to me one afternoon in our long whitewashed dairy, where I was busy upon some task, and telling me in a low voice that he had definitely come to the conclusion he must marry X. A sense of horror came over me, and I said bitterly:

'Then all that has been, all that we are to one another will be wiped out, like rubbing writing off a slate.'

'Nothing need be rubbed off, but the other thing, it *has* to be,' he hissed. My new bicycle was leaning against the wall, and the bright steel hurt me like a blow. I suddenly thought:

'Life is rich indeed if it gives you a second time what I have to give.'

Soon afterwards Lawrence wrote to me that X. was to spend a week-end in Croydon, staying as a guest of the family with whom he lodged, as his sister, and myself, and other friends had done. In his letter the following week he said, 'X. was here for the week-end, but it's no good. Somehow as soon as I am alone with her I want to run away.' And the project was mentioned no more.

LITERARY DÉBUT

LAWRENCE and I first talked about the publication of his work, so far as I remember, on a cold evening in the spring of 1908, when he had been bringing his writings to me for two years. It was nearly the end of his last term in College and there was the sense of an impending break and a new point of departure. He was in one of his still, indrawn moods, he had been going to the dentist and was feeling a little out of sorts. The sky was a leaden colour and the green of the wood and fields showed intense in the dull light. He was telling me in a quiet and deliberately unexpressive voice that he had sent some of his work to an author, whose weekly article in the *Daily News* we often read and discussed, asking him if he would give his opinion as to its merit. I had not heard of this before and I cannot be sure whether the work in question was a story or an essay, but I am inclined to think it was the latter. Some weeks or even months had passed since he sent it, and now he was telling me that the author's wife had returned the manuscript, saying that her husband regretted his inability to give an opinion, owing to pressure of work.

'So evidently,' said Lawrence, 'his wife acts as his amanuensis.'

I recognized only too well the chagrin that lay behind his casual words. I murmured something sympathetic and Lawrence continued in the same flat voice:

'I've tried, and been turned down, and I shall try no more. And I don't care if I never have a line published,' he concluded in a tone of finality. I said nothing, knowing it was futile to argue with him in his present mood. But I began to wonder what would become of him if he should fail to get a hearing.

We never referred to the incident again. Lawrence continued to bring, and when he left home to send his writings to me: poems frequently, and always the novel which ultimately became *The White Peacock*. It was at Christmas of this year on his first holiday from Croydon that he showed us the *English Review* for December, 1908. We were delighted with the journal. The very look of it, with its fine blue cover and handsome black type, was satisfying. Father thoroughly appreciated it, and we decided to subscribe to it amongst us. The coming of the *English Review* into our lives was an event, one of the few really first-rate things that happen now and again in a lifetime. I remember what a joy it was to get the solid, handsome journal from our local newsagent, and feel it was a link with the world of literature. I soon noticed that the Editor was prepared to welcome new talent. I drew Lawrence's attention to this and begged him to submit some of his work, but he refused absolutely. I asked what was to become of his writing if he made no attempt to place any of it.

'I don't care what becomes of it,' he said stubbornly. 'I'm not anxious to get into print. I shan't send anything. Besides they'd never take it.'

'How do you know unless you try?' I persisted, and he suddenly said:

'*You* send something. Send some of the poems, if you like.'

'Very well, which shall I send?'

'Send whatever you like. Do what you like with them,' he answered. Then, seeing I was in earnest, he added: 'Give me a *nom de plume*, though; I don't want folk in Croydon to know I write poetry.' And he would say nothing more.

I looked through the poems Lawrence had sent in letters to me since he left home, picked out what I thought were the best, and copied them out one beautiful June morning. I was careful to put the poem called 'Discipline' first, not because I thought it was the best, but hoping that the unusual title might attract the Editor's attention. In 'Dreams Old and Nascent' I knew he was trying to explain himself to me; and 'Baby Movements' I sent because I loved it. It was about the baby in the family with whom he lived in Croydon. He was very fond of her and often spoke about her in letters. I enclosed also several other poems whose titles I don't remember. I wrote a letter to the Editor of the *English Review* saying that the author of the poems was a young man who had been writing for a number of years, and who would be very grateful for any recognition. I gave his name, of course, but said that if any of the poems were printed they should appear under the *nom de plume* of Richard Greasley (Richards was an unacknowledged name of Lawrence's, and Greasley was his home parish). The next time I saw Lawrence he said:

'Did you send those poems to the *English*?' adding immediately, 'They'll never print them.'

The reply came in August when the Lawrences were on holiday at Shanklin in the Isle of Wight. It said, as nearly as I can remember, that the poems were very interesting and that the author had undoubted talent, but that nowadays luck played such a large part in a literary career, and continued, 'If you would get him to come and see me some time when he is in London perhaps something might be done.' The letter was signed Ford Madox Hueffer, a name that I knew only in connection with the first instalment of the serial story, *A Call*, in the current number of the *English Review*. I replied that Mr. Lawrence was away at the moment, but when school re-opened I was sure he would be glad to call on Mr. Hueffer.

Lawrence wrote to me from Shanklin, a long descriptive letter about the island and the fun they all had bathing, but I kept my news until he returned. When we were alone together I said:

'Oh, I've got a letter for you.'

He looked at me quickly, then his eyes narrowed:

'From the *English*? About the poems? Show it me.'

I gave him the letter, and his face became tense.

'*You* are my luck,' he murmured. Then he said with suppressed excitement, 'Let me take it to show mother.' And I never saw it again.

In our talks that holiday Lawrence told me that his mother and sister were not pleased with him. He was changing, they said, and breaking away from the old things, and they hated him to be different from what he used to be. He felt it was hard and narrow on their part. He had to change, and leave the old things, but he thought they might go on liking him just the same.

As I had not been away for a holiday I reminded Lawrence of the project for making up a party and visiting the historic remains of Nottingham. He looked worried for a moment, but said he would like it, adding, 'The others probably won't want to, so if we go *à deux*, we go *à deux*.' It was arranged that the party (if there was one) should meet at his home. When I called Lawrence was not ready, and his sister was nowhere to be seen. I asked Mrs. Lawrence if A. was to accompany us, and she replied shortly that she was not. I thought Mrs. Lawrence might make some reference to Hueffer's letter, but she said nothing. I seemed to be in disgrace. At the time I could not understand why, and I can only surmise that Lawrence in self-defence told his mother I had sent the poems without his knowledge, so that in her eyes I was guilty of unwarrantable interference in his affairs. Whatever the reason, the atmosphere suggested an imminent thunderstorm. I tried to take no notice and went on talking, only to feel the air grow more oppressive. We set off finally with the distinct sense of a rod in pickle, for either or both of us.

As was usual when the home atmosphere was disturbed in this way, Lawrence took refuge in an arrogance which I felt to be a mask for his own wretchedness. I tried not to be affected by it, but after a time my spirit flagged and I became a mere bundle of misery. It was the same at the café where we had tea. Lawrence's precise and distant manner withered my attempts at conversation. Afterwards he strode along to one of the picturesque old shops near the Castle, where he bought some photographs of Greek statuary. One was 'Amor et Psyche', which he said ominously was for me. The remainder of the evening is a blank in my memory, but we must have been to a theatre, because it was late when we went home. I was to stay with my sister (who was now married) and on the walk from the station Lawrence poured out his accumulated spleen. It was the old story. There could never, *never* be anything between us but an association of the mind and the spirit. I was Psyche, I was the soul, and I had no other significance for him . . . But it was uttered with the dehumanized vehemence that was so devastating. At the gate he held out the picture of 'Amor et Psyche'.

'Take it,' he said, 'it is you. You are Psyche, you are the soul, and I leave you, as I *must*.' He gazed at me for a moment with a face set in agony, then turned on his heel and began to stamp his way homeward. I felt terror-stricken, for both of us, but more for him. I ran for some steps after him and called, but his heel rang on the pavement so that it was impossible for him to hear me. I went back to the cottage.

In the morning I felt too ill to go home. My sister mercifully asked no questions, and later in the day we returned together. I learned afterwards that Lawrence arrived at the cottage soon after we had gone, and badly wanted to start in pursuit of us. He was assured that he could not overtake us, and remained hanging about, moody and silent.

On the following day I was myself again. I decided that to continue in this way was sheer waste of life. So I cycled into Nottingham and called at the Education Offices, asking to be placed in a school in the town so that I could study in the evenings at the University.

I was sitting over a late tea when Lawrence walked into the kitchen. In the town I had bought Arnold Bennett's *A Great Man*, and was reading it with huge enjoyment. I glanced up and gave him a casual greeting. He replied stiffly and sat down on the sofa, facing me. I resumed my reading. My brother got ready and went out to meet his fiancée. I could feel Lawrence

getting more and more rigid, and said to him laugh-
ingly:

'You don't mind my going on reading, do you?
This is really funny.'

'Not at all,' he replied. I returned to my book, but
after a while Lawrence's misery began to invade me,
as it always did.

'I shall have to go soon,' he said in a quiet voice. 'I
didn't bring a lamp.'

'You can borrow mine,' I rejoined, and began to
read again. He made a movement to go.

'Are you in a hurry?' I asked.

'Not particularly,' he replied, miserably.

'Well, I'll make some coffee soon.' Something
seemed to reach father behind his newspaper.

'You may as well have a bit of supper while you're
here,' he said.

I made coffee and told Lawrence what I had done in
Nottingham, and the misery went out of his face.
Presently I fetched the lamp from my bicycle.

'Walk a little way with me, there won't be another
chance,' he said. It was a perfect night, and I walked
with him along the high road and down Hunt's hill.
At the field path I stopped.

'You *might* come a bit farther,' he pleaded. 'You
know there'll be an awful row if I'm late, but nobody
will say a word to you.'

I walked on, carrying the bicycle lamp in my hand.
We talked of one thing and another, but as all paths

lead to Rome, our conversation inevitably led back to the theme, which seemed to have become an obsession with him, of how and whom he should marry. Each time I stopped to turn back he begged me to go a little farther. Finally, when I had walked nearly as far as his home, he said desperately:

'It isn't that I don't want to marry. I'd marry to-morrow, if I could only find someone I *could* marry. I'd marry *you* if only I could. As I am at present I shall go from woman to woman until I am satisfied.' I looked at him in horror and compassion. He was so clearly in the grip of a tension he could not control, that seemed to pull him in opposite directions with equal force. I could say nothing, and left him. I crossed the field path in the soft starlight, and when I had passed through the Warren and come into our own fields I stayed for a long time watching the stars and listening to the silence. It was midnight when I went to the house. My brother had just bolted the door. He was astonished to see me there with the bicycle lamp in my hand.

Lawrence went to see Ford Madox Hueffer in September and wrote to me: '. . . He is fairish, fat, about forty, and the kindest man on earth.' Hueffer introduced him to various literary and artistic people, and meeting them excited and tired him very much. He wrote:

'Last night I dined with celebrities, and to-night I am dining with two R.A.s, but I'd give it all up for one of our old evenings in the Haggs parlour.' Some of the poems I had sent were to be published in the November number of the *English Review*. Hueffer interested himself also in Lawrence's novel.

In a later letter he said:

'It is snowing, and I ought to be out on Wimbledon Common with a girl, a teacher here . . . I have almost made up my mind to marry her as soon as I get some money. I think I shall. I am almost sure I shall.'

In a further letter he told me that his sister complained that he went about too much and did not send money home. 'But then,' he wrote, 'I am in digs. I can't hang about the house as if I were at home.'

Soon after the meeting with Hueffer, Lawrence began begging me to go and see him in London. He had so much to tell me and to show me. He had written a play, and there were poems it was 'too much fag' to copy out. He also wanted me to meet the girl he had almost decided to marry . . . With the memory of our last outing still fresh in my mind, I told him I didn't want to go. But he became urgent, and at last I promised to go at the end of November. Lawrence met me at King's Cross and as soon as we were seated on the top of a bus, he told me that Hueffer had made him promise to take me to see him when I came to London. My heart sank, for I dreaded meeting strangers.

'I told him,' said Lawrence, 'I must get you here in London before I let you know, or you'd never come.'

'I never would,' I replied, 'but of course I'll go now I'm here.'

I banished all thought of it, lest it should cast a shadow on the day. Lawrence was in a genial mood, and London was a place of wonder. He took me first to see the big shops, and I felt how trivial was all the wealth they displayed compared with the joy of being with him. We had lunch at Selfridge's and Lawrence sent a postcard to his possible fiancée telling her that he would take me to see her in the morning.

'Will she really like to see me?' I asked.

'Oh yes, she's keen on seeing you,' he answered. 'She thought herself great shakes until she met me and heard about you.'

'Why, what has she done?'

'Well, her mother's an awful tyrant of the strict Sabbatarian variety, so she left home and struck out for herself.'

From Selfridge's we went to the National Gallery, and when night came on he took me to Waterloo Bridge and made me look at the human wreckage preparing to spend the night on the Embankment. He wanted me to see the bridges at night, with the lights of the trams reflected, as he had described them in his poems. Finally we went to a theatre, and in the steep gallery, sitting between Lawrence and a negro, I watched a play called *The Making of a Gentleman*. The negro was so still, I wondered what he thought of it. Lawrence explained to me that the theatre existed mainly in the interests of fashion, and that the leaders of Society came not for the play (which was obviously rubbish) but to observe the varied and beautiful dresses worn by the leading ladies.

When we reached his lodgings the family had gone to bed. Once inside the house Lawrence glowed. As he was hanging up my things I asked him if he liked my hat, and he replied:

'It's the very blue I've always so admired.'

He took a saucepan from the hearth.

'I'm awfully sorry, it's macaroni again,' he said. We had had macaroni at lunch. But it didn't matter. We could have banqueted on a crust. Supper over, he cleared the table and began to show me his writings. There were poems, quite a number that I had not seen, and a play that was about his home on a Friday night. Sitting there in the tiny suburban room, it troubled me deeply to see his home put before me in his vivid phrases. He was watching me keenly:

'Do you like it?' he asked.

'It's very true. But let me take it home. I can't read properly here.' He swept the papers together.

'Now we'll talk,' he said. 'But perhaps you want to go to bed?' It was one o'clock. I had left home at six the morning before. 'Can you stay up a little longer? Can you give me one hour?' he asked.

'Yes, I can stay another hour,' I answered.

Then he began to ask me very earnestly — What did I expect from life, what did I hope for in the future?

I bent my head and the tears ran down into my lap,
because in my heart was no hope at all, but only
fortitude. So I said:

'I don't know. I can't tell. I don't hope for anything much. But I shall get along somehow. I'm not
afraid.'

He looked hard at me, thinking deeply. Then he
began to tell me what a terrible strain he found the
new life, the excitement, and the meeting with such
different people. He said how hard it was to bear the
stress of life alone, and how much he needed to be
married. He said softly:

'You know, I could so easily peg out.' In my mind
I saw a candle puffed out in a gust of wind.

'Well,' I said, not entirely without irony, 'you have
only to make a choice.'

'Have I?' he asked, and sat thinking. 'But I've no
money,' he went on. 'I shan't be able to marry for ever
so long. I think I shall ask some girl if she will give
me . . . that . . . without marriage. Do you think any
girl would?'

'I don't know,' I answered. 'The kind of girl who
would, I think you wouldn't like.'

'Would you think it wrong?'

'No, I wouldn't think it wrong. But all the girls I
know would.'

'But *you* wouldn't?' he insisted.

'Not *wrong*. But it would be very difficult.'

He seemed to hang upon my words. Compassion

for him brought to my mind: 'Whoso giveth a cup of cold water in My name . . .' After a pause he said:

'Well, I think I shall ask *her*. Do you think she would?'

'It depends how much she is in love with you,' I replied. He sat deep in thought. I reminded him of the time.

'Look, Bert, it's two o'clock. I really am tired now.'

'It's two o'clock,' he repeated; 'it's two o'clock. *Must* you go to bed?'

'Yes, I must go now,' I said, getting up from my chair.

'Very well. I'll let you go. You shall go,' he said.

In the morning we went to see his friend. She was tall, with grey eyes and auburn hair. She was pleasant — and a school-mistress. She talked to Lawrence rather like an elder sister, and there was about him the curious air of bravado that I always felt arose from lack of conviction. I could only marvel at the inscrutable ruling of fate. She greeted me warmly and pinned a spray of red berries in my coat. Lawrence made an assignation with her and we took our leave.

We were to go first to Hueffer's flat in Holland Park, and then to Violet Hunt's house in Kensington to lunch. With the spectacle of London's opulence before us Lawrence exclaimed:

'I'll make two thousand a year!'

'Will you?' I said indifferently. I didn't care whether he made two thousand pounds or two thousand pence. I had never imagined Lawrence making money. I thought he would aim at something finer and more original. The name Holland Park suggested a Dutch atmosphere and open space and trees; so I felt slightly bewildered to find only streets and houses. In the flat there were piles of the *English Review* lying on the black polished floor and on the window-seat. Lawrence told me that Hueffer was very fond of this flat and said he felt a sense of satisfaction every time he entered it.

'I can't say I should,' said Lawrence critically. He nodded towards a photograph on the mantelpiece. 'Violet Hunt', he whispered. At that moment Hueffer came into the room. I looked up at him, intent on seeing what manner of man he was who was going to make such a difference in Lawrence's life, but his own penetrating gaze made me drop my eyes. For some moments he stood smiling down at me and chatting. It was not until he said, indicating the portrait of a small boy hanging over the mantelpiece, 'That is a portrait of me as a little boy, painted by my grand-father,' that I was able to look up again. I glanced at the portrait of the chubby, rosy-cheeked boy, and at Hueffer and said I liked it; but the thought that flashed through my mind was, 'Ah — you were fat even as a child.' Hueffer smiled at me, and Lawrence gave a short, half-derisive laugh. Here Hueffer unpinned a paper and showed me an announcement of a Suffragette meeting.

'I suppose you're interested in that,' he said.

'Oh, yes, I've a very enthusiastic friend who tells me all about it,' I replied. Then a little later he said:

'You're a sort of Socialist, I suppose?'

Not a single political idea had crossed my mind in those days; but I liked the pleasant ambiguity of his definition and decided there and then that it described me exactly. He told me he had two votes, but had never voted once, and never would, until women also were able to vote. This sounded like knight-errantry I thought.

We set off to walk to the house in Kensington, and I remarked how strange it was that a place never looked as one expected it would.

'How did you expect it would look?' Hueffer asked in an eager voice.

I was suddenly self-conscious and murmured that I could never have imagined an avenue without trees. I was shy, but not so shy as to be insensible to the charm with which Hueffer was talking to me. I suppose never before or since has anyone talked to me with quite such charm, making me feel in the most delicate way that what I said was of interest. I found myself telling him that I lived not even in a village, but at an isolated farm behind a wood. He answered that to him that part of London always seemed like a village, because he had watched it grow from a village

since his boyhood. I told him about the autumn shooting parties in the wood, and how afterwards the game-
keepers would bring us a brace of pheasants and
partridges, and perhaps a hare.

So by the time we arrived at our destination I had
completely got over my shyness, and was entering into
the situation and enjoying it. Hueffer's pleasant
manner in addressing the maid-servant who opened the
door to us was not lost on me. It confirmed my impression of genuine kindliness. The maid took me
upstairs to what was evidently her mistress's study
where I left my outdoor things. Then she conducted
me to the drawing-room and announced me under a
wrong name.

Violet Hunt greeted me cordially. Lawrence had
warned me that she would perhaps not shake hands —
people in that sphere of society sometimes didn't, he
said — but she shook hands with me and introduced
me to the other people in the room: her mother — an
old, old lady — and a young American poet who
startled me by springing to his feet and bowing from
the waist with the stiff precision of a mechanical toy.
There was also a quiet man named Byles, who had
joined us on the way, and who bowed to me, smiling,
from his chair.

At lunch I sat between the American poet and Mr.
Byles, with Hueffer and Lawrence opposite, and the
two ladies at either end of the table. I noted the excellent cooking — how the gravy ran down into the

dish when Violet Hunt carved the joint, and brussel sprouts I never had seen so perfectly cooked — each one sound and whole. Our hostess told us that the plum pudding was one from the Christmas before, and I thoroughly enjoyed the simple, homely fare.

The young American poet was the life of the party. He flung out observations in an abrupt way that reminded me of his poetry:

'Why do you give us solid stuff like roast beef and plum pudding for lunch?' And later, 'Shall I show you how an American eats an apple?'

He speared an apple with his knife, chopped it into quarters and gobbled it ostentatiously. I regarded him as an amiable buffoon. Hueffer remarked to me that Mr. Byles had once lived on a small holding, but it was obvious to me that he had never had to depend upon a small holding for his living—he was too suave and urbane.

Somebody mentioned Carlyle and Ruskin, and Lawrence admitted that he had read them both.

'You're the only man I've ever met,' said Hueffer, 'who really has read all those people.'

We said we had seen Galsworthy's *Strife* in the theatre at Nottingham. Hueffer asked me if I liked it. He looked sceptical when I said I did. Religion was mentioned, and Lawrence remarked that we had both been brought up as Congregationalists. Mr. Byles said he, too, was a Congregationalist, whereupon Hueffer smiled and said that all the nice young people he knew nowadays seemed to be Congregationalists.

The talk turned to the Suffragettes. Violet Hunt told us that such things were done to the women who were taken to prison as they wouldn't even tell their friends. A favourite form of torture was to hold a lighted match inside the hand. . . . When prison was mentioned the young poet looked round and said that for his part he had never in his life been inside a room that reminded him more of a prison than the one he was in at the moment. . . .

I suddenly felt tired and wished it was time to go. I looked at Lawrence sitting so straight and alert, and thought that this was perhaps the last of our days together. A wave of melancholy swept over me. I could see so well the wonderful man he might be if only the deep reserves in his nature could be truly liberated . . . The conversation pattered around me like raindrops, and at last the interminable meal came to an end.

In the drawing-room Violet Hunt said she thought she had seen my handwriting — hadn't I sent some poems of Lawrence's to the *English Review*? I said I had, and how delighted we were to have Mr. Hueffer's reply. Then she exclaimed:

'But you *discovered* him.' To which I replied that we had been acquainted with one another ever since we were hardly more than children.

Presently the gentlemen came in. The American poet continued to rattle off his questions like a succession of squibs. Finally he put a question to Hueffer that electrified me.

'How would *you* speak to a working man?' he asked. 'Would you speak to him just the same as to any other man, or would you make a difference?' I nearly held my breath for the answer. Perhaps Hueffer found my gaze embarrassing, because he hesitated a moment and glanced at me before he said:

'I should speak to a working man in exactly the same way that I should speak to any other man, because I don't think there is any difference.'

I don't know whether my face glowed, but I certainly was aglow inside, because I felt he was sincere. Yet more than ever I longed to go. When someone asked what time it was, I took the opportunity of saying that I must be at King's Cross at four. Soon we all rose, and Violet Hunt took me into her study to put my things on. She was extremely kind. She said that Mr. Hueffer would do all he could for Lawrence, and they would both talk about his novel to their friends.

I felt uncomfortable in what I saw was a false situation. Violet Hunt and Hueffer obviously looked upon Lawrence and me as at least a virtually engaged couple. When she commented upon the red berries in my coat I told her that a lady friend of Mr. Lawrence's had pinned them there. It was on the tip of my tongue to say: 'She is the lady Mr. Lawrence thinks he may marry.'

Hueffer walked along with Lawrence and me for quite a distance.

'Why don't you come and teach in London?' he asked me. Lawrence explained that the London education authorities preferred to employ their own teachers. He had shown Hueffer a little sketch of mine. Hueffer liked it, and asked me what else I was doing. He told me I wrote nicely, but must be careful to keep off high-falutin, which was damnable. Then he suggested I should write something about myself, and Lawrence put in:

'It wouldn't be any good. She's incommunicable.'

Hueffer looked at me and laughed:

'There you are, you see, labelled, put away on the shelf, and done with.' He advised me to go on writing and send anything I did to him, and he might be able to help me. His kindliness impressed me and I thanked him sincerely. Indeed, whenever I recollect that leisurely Sunday afternoon walk through the grey November murk — with Lawrence almost skipping to accommodate his impatient steps to our slow ones — I feel again the genial warmth of Hueffer's personality.

When he had left us Lawrence exclaimed in a sort of nervous exasperation:

'Isn't he fat, and doesn't he walk *slow*! He says he walks about London two hours every day to keep his fat down. But he won't keep much down if he always walks at that pace.'

I replied that he was wonderfully kind.

'Oh, he's kind, he's *kind*,' Lawrence agreed. Then he suddenly asked me how I liked having champagne with my lunch. I said I didn't know it was champagne, but that anyhow I liked it. Then he said:

'Did you hear where Hueffer said he was going next?' [This was in answer to a question from Violet Hunt.] 'He was going to see Lady ———,' Lawrence continued with a significant glance. It seemed extraordinary to me that a man with his gifts should care about the kind of 'distinction' that titles confer. He knew how I felt. On an earlier occasion he had said:

'How that glittering taketh me,' was true of himself.

'Does it?' I had replied. 'I'm afraid it doesn't take me.'

'I know,' and he hung his head. 'But . . . it does me . . .'

My train went in a few minutes. Lawrence raced along the platform for my rug. Then he said:

'If you are going down to Eastwood in the week, you might call and tell mother about it. She'll like to hear how we went on.'

I promised I would. He gave me his play to read, and stood close to the carriage window until the train began to move. Suddenly I saw that he was deeply agitated.

I went to see Lawrence's mother one evening. She listened with a supercilious air while I told her briefly about the meeting with Hueffer and Violet Hunt. When I had finished she said almost genially:

'Well, it would be very interesting.'

I asked her if she liked the poems that had been published in the *English Review*.

'Yes, I did like them,' she answered, still slightly on the defensive. 'I thought they were heaps better than that by John Lazerus.'

'And did you like Hueffer's story *A Call*?'

'I did. But I wondered how he was going to end it.' Then she said significantly, 'When two women are both in love with the same man, one of them usually has to be disappointed.'

She looked into my face searchingly. I knew what she meant, but I returned her gaze with unflinching candour, and replied as if casually, 'It is so. In a case like that someone usually is disappointed.' She held my eyes for a moment, searching for a clue, then turned away baffled.

I had only one care, that no one should guess I was hurt. It was a comfort to remember that changes were afoot. I was going to teach in a big town school in the New Year. My family also was leaving the farm and going to one nearer the town. I was glad to be leaving the valley, that I had completely outgrown, and almost come to hate. I expected that Lawrence would marry the auburn-haired teacher, and tried to accustom myself to the idea. He had said to me many times, vehemently:

'It doesn't matter *who* one marries.'

'SONS AND LOVERS'

The Christmas of 1910 provided the greatest possible contrast to the Christmas of the year before. It was hard to believe that such a complete change could come about within the space of a single year. Life then was rich with promise, and opening out to wonderful possibilities. Lawrence's poems had been published in the *English Review* and his novel, *The White Peacock*, the writing of which had served as his apprenticeship to the craft of literature, was receiving sympathetic consideration. He told us, knowing how we should appreciate the valuation, that some of the descriptions of nature were considered equal to those in Hardy's *Tess of the D'Urbervilles*.

A new and immensely larger life was opening out before him. A kind of transfiguration from obscurity and uncertainty had taken place. Thanks to the kind offices of Ford Madox Hueffer his chance of a hearing was assured. And it had all come about so simply, almost without effort. There was a glamour about those days, even something of a glitter. It made me feel dizzy, as though the foundations that had always seemed so firm were rocking slightly. A faint atmosphere of unreality suggested to me that I was indeed the Lady of Shalott as Lawrence liked to hint I was, and saw only the reflection of things in a mirror.

It was at Christmas, 1909, that he made the great attempt to resolve the conflict in himself. Soon after my return from London he sent me the verse 'Aware', but I had always been careful not to take his poems too literally. Now he came to me and told me that he had been mistaken all these years, that he must have loved me all along without knowing it. The idea of marrying the Croydon teacher was a mistake. He had told her so, he said, and everything was over between them, and in fact she left Croydon shortly afterwards, and passed out of his life. The years of our friendship had been simply a preparation for this, he said, and he hadn't known before. But we wouldn't speak of it to anyone yet. They would make such a fuss and ask so many questions. It should be our secret for the present. We would go our own way and say nothing to anyone for a while. . . .

In spite of myself I heard the old forced note, the need to convince himself. But I felt how sincere was his desire to be convinced. And on my side was the bond of love, and the long loyalty.

That was the Christmas of 1909. When Christmas came round again that world was shattered. We had lived through a year of successive crises, of which the culminating one was the death of Lawrence's mother.

The early months of the year were spent in the final revision of *The White Peacock*, which was finished in a

rare sunny mood. Asking me to help him to find a
title (for the story had hitherto been called 'Nethermere'), Lawrence wrote: 'I have always believed it
was the woman who paid the price in life. But I've
made a discovery. It's the man who pays, not the
woman.'

On a day in the Easter holiday he said to me: 'I
thought you would be sure to write some day, but now
I begin to ha'e ma doots . . . You have a *wonderful*
sympathy, and perhaps that's your gift. I think God
intended you to make a *good* wife — and not much more.
Do you mind?'

I replied that I was well content.

Towards the end of the same holiday he was
planning his next novel. He told me he would write a
'bright' story, and take one of my brothers (the
Maurice of *Love Among the Haystacks*) as hero. Almost
immediately on returning to Croydon he wrote,
apparently very much disturbed, saying that he found
he had to write the story of Siegmund . . . It was
in front of him and he had got to do it. He begged
me to go to Croydon and make the acquaintance of
'Helen'.

His second novel, *The Trespasser*, was written in
feverish haste between the Whitsuntide and Mid-
summer of 1910. Lawrence implored me not to
attempt to hold him. He told me most impressively
the story of the Shirt of Nessus. Something of that
kind, he said, something fatal, perhaps, might happen

if I insisted on holding him: 'For this I need Helen, but I must *always* return to you,' he said earnestly, 'only you must always leave me free.'

When the August holiday came Lawrence suggested that he should spend some days with our family at the new farm, which he had scarcely seen, and we prepared a room for him. He went home first, however, and when I met him several days later, instead of returning with me as he had planned to do, he broke off our engagement completely. He had returned, overnight as it were, to his old attitude. Letters arrived at the farm for him during the week, so the change of mood must have occurred after he left Croydon.

I stood, as always, for complete union or a complete break. I could not move from my old standpoint of all or nothing, even when Lawrence said: 'Then I am afraid it must be nothing.' We agreed not even to correspond. Within a week there came an importunate note from him:

'*Do* read Barrie's *Sentimental Tommy* and *Tommy and Grizel*. I've just had them out of the library here. They'll help you to understand how it is with me. I'm in exactly the same predicament.'

Before the holiday was over I had a pathetic message, telling me of his mother's illness, that was to prove fatal.

The autumn of his mother's dying imposed a terrible strain upon Lawrence. He was never the same man again. He came home on alternate week-ends to be with her. I saw him several times, and although he was superficially interested in things one could not help feeling how terribly alone he was in his grief. Love was unavailing, no matter how sincere or how selfless. In his presence one felt only the horror of sheer hopelessness. His mother's death completed the break-up of the old life, that had proved so rich in experience and achievement.

A fortnight or so before his mother's death I had occasion to call at the village post office and a letter from Lawrence was handed to me. In the dim light I read: 'I was in the train with X. on Saturday and I suddenly asked her to marry me. I never meant to. But she accepted me and I shall stick to it. I've written to her father . . . I'll go over the old ground again, if you like, and explain. Do you want me to say little, or nothing, or much? I'll say anything you like, only I can't help it, I'm made this way.'

Lawrence was with his mother when she died. He sent word to me, and on a Sunday morning, the day before her funeral, we met and walked once more on the familiar lanes. As we passed the reservoir a beggar whined for alms. Lawrence brutally tossed a coin to him, and the man grovelled for it in the dust. I looked at Lawrence in anger, and he answered:

'Yes, a man has sunk pretty low when he can take a copper in that fashion.'

I told him he had done wrong to involve X. in the

impasse of our relationship: 'You should not have
drawn X. into things,' I said. 'She has no idea of the
real state of affairs.'

'With *should* and *ought* I have nothing to do,' Lawrence replied coldly. We walked on in anguish of
spirit. At the railway track leading down to the pits
we remained standing a long time. We seemed to be
completely shut in by the grey December day, quite
removed from the world of human contact. Suddenly
out of the gloom a collier appeared on his way to work.
He had a red scarf round his neck and a tea-can was
sticking out of his pocket. He looked at us with
startled eyes. Lawrence glanced at him as he passed.

'There you are,' he said, 'A story by Chekhov —
"The Man in the Red Muffler".'

We waited some time longer, then Lawrence looked
at me with intensity. 'You know — I've always loved
mother,' he said in a strangled voice.

'I know you have,' I replied.

'I don't mean that,' he returned quickly. 'I've *loved*
her, like a lover. That's why I could never love you.'

With that he silently gave me a draft of the poems
he had just written: 'The End', 'The Bride', 'The
Virgin Mother'.

After his mother's death Lawrence was like a rudder-
less ship — 'a leaf blown in the wind' — was his
favourite simile for himself.

Throughout the following year I saw him on fewer

occasions than I could count on the fingers of one hand, but he begged me to write to him:

'Write to me whenever you feel like it,' he urged in a letter. 'Don't wait for it to be your turn, but write whenever you feel you have something to say.'

Early in the year I had a letter in which he said: 'I am not strong like you. You can fight your battle and have done with it, but I *have* to run away, or I couldn't bear things. I have to fight a bit, and then run away, and then fight a bit more. So I really do go on fighting, only it has to be at intervals . . . At times I am afflicted by a perversity amounting to minor insanity. But the best man in me belongs to you. One me is yours, a fine, strong me . . . I have great faith still that things will come right in the end.'

This was during the year of his engagement to X.

The situation was simply that his mother had claimed his love, all the spontaneous tenderness without which 'love' is a mockery. And having given it to her fully and unreservedly Lawrence had in truth no love to give anyone else, so that his agonized reiteration of his inability to love me was nothing but a bare statement of fact. It was the ineluctable position in which he found himself.

It was difficult to understand this, in those days, but it was what Lawrence meant when he offered to 'go over the ground again and explain'. The incredible thing was the exclusiveness, and the incapacitating nature of the mother-love.

I could not bring myself to believe that the situation was irreparable. I wanted to make the effect of his mother's attitude clear to him. It seemed to me that our long conflict had dated from the time when, as a boy of twenty, he had come to me and told me that 'he had looked into his heart and could not find that he loved me as a husband should love his wife'. So I recollected the incidents of that occasion with scrupulous care and sent them to him in the form of a short story some time in the spring of 1911.

I knew what I had done must pain him, but I thought it was a pain that might lead to health. His answer came promptly: 'I have read your story but I don't think you'll get anyone to publish it with alacrity; it's too subtle . . .' Then his pose of detachment broke down: 'You say you died a death of me,' he wrote, 'but the death you died of me I must have died also, or you wouldn't have gone on caring about me . . . They tore me from you, the love of my life . . . It was the slaughter of the fœtus in the womb . . .' The concluding sentence of the letter ran, 'I've got a grinning skull-and-crossbones headache. The amount of energy required to live is — how many volts a second?'

I saw Lawrence in the October of that year when 'Helen' and I were at a theatre in London at the same time as he and his brother. Our seats were not together, but Lawrence came to speak to us during the interval. He looked frail and insubstantial. It was obvious that he was living under a severe strain. He sat beside me in the train that took us to Croydon. I asked him if he was not well. I was aware of a sudden relaxation of his defensive attitude, but he replied that he was all right. Then he said that perhaps he wasn't very well . . . and was silent for some moments. It was then that he spoke to me for the first time of Edward Garnett, saying how friendly he was. He said that Garnett's philosophy was: 'Follow the gleam.'

'That's all very well when a man's middle-aged and static,' Lawrence said with a touch of bitterness. 'But when you're young it's not always easy to know what *is* the gleam.'

It was impossible not to see that he was profoundly unhappy. There seemed to be a central core of suffering from which he could not escape. And the tragedy of it was that nobody could help him. Beyond being humanly kind as one would be to any fellow-creature in pain, one could do nothing. He was like a man set apart. Only Lawrence might help himself. Anyone else was powerless. His salvation, if it was possible at all, lay within himself. But before he could achieve it he had to realize the nature of his malady. He did realize it in part, and in sudden flashes. But his instinct was to evade it, to run away, as he said. His engagement to X. was an attempt to evade the dilemma that faced him. If appearance counted for anything, however, evasion was an inadequate solution.

When I returned on the Sunday evening Lawrence's

brother travelled along with me. He had been a married man with a family ever since I had been acquainted with him, and he talked to me like an elder brother.

'He isn't at all well,' he said, referring to Lawrence. 'He calls out in his sleep, thinks somebody's trying to kill him. And he's such a pessimist, too. Over this war scare [the Agadir incident] he says it's a pity it didn't come to war. He wishes it had. "Let 'em fight", he said. "What does it matter?" '

I read in this only Lawrence's despair. The spontaneous flow of his life was checked and turned inwards destructively. My companion spoke of his brother's engagement, and I asked him if he thought they would get married soon. He stared at me incredulously.

'Married!' he ejaculated. 'I don't *think*, I *know* they'll never get married. Why, how d'you suppose he let me know about his engagement?' he went on scornfully. 'On a blooming postcard. He brought her to see us. "Well, what d'you think of her?" he said. "Oh, she's all right. A nice girl, very kind when mother was ill, I know. But you've got the wrong girl", I said to him. "Oh, do you think so," he said, "I don't." But they'll never get married, never in this world,' he concluded.

The situation would have been more bearable if Lawrence had looked happy, if there had been any prospect that the issue would be fortunate. But as things were it seemed to be simply a case of waiting for the breaking point. And the memory of Lawrence's face, with its white look of obstinacy, made one feel how bitter and protracted that breaking point would be.

The publication of *The White Peacock* early that year came as a kind of anticlimax to the writing of it. Lawrence sent me a copy with a verse on the fly-leaf saying he was like a leaf blown in the wind. I don't know whether its publication brought any joy to him, but I, who had shared so closely in the making of the book: — 'I its creator, you its nurse', he had written to me — had to swallow a lump when someone told me that his fiancée was handing it round to her acquaintances as the work of the clever young author to whom she was engaged. The irony of the situation made me laugh, however. It was literally too funny for words.

Lawrence never gave me the impression that he thought much of *The White Peacock*.

'It's a first novel,' he used to say deprecatingly. 'Publishers take no notice of a first novel. They know that nearly anybody can write one novel, if he can write at all, because it's about himself. A second novel's a step further. It's the third that counts, though. That's the *pons asinorum* of the novelist. If he can get over that ass's bridge he's a writer, he can go on.'

His second novel, *The Trespasser*, was done rapidly. It was something so apart from our lives that Lawrence spoke to me of it very little. The only discussion I remember was about the Doppelgänger. He asked me what I thought about that part of the story. He went on to say meditatively how a passion might suck a man down into a vortex. It was a more intense form of the old fear that he had told me about when he had been so upset by Sarah Bernhardt in *La Dame aux Camelias*.

Lawrence began to write his autobiographical novel during 1911, which was perhaps the most arid year of his life. He did not tell me himself that he was at work upon this theme. I heard of it through 'Helen'. He had been working on it for the greater part of the year, and it was some time after our brief meeting in October that he sent the entire manuscript to me, and asked me to tell him what I thought of it.

He had written about two-thirds of the story, and seemed to have come to a standstill. The whole thing was somehow tied up. The characters were locked together in a frustrating bondage, and there seemed no way out. The writing oppressed me with a sense of strain. It was extremely tired writing. I was sure that Lawrence had had to force himself to do it. The spontaneity that I had come to regard as the distinguishing feature of his writing was quite lacking. He was telling the story of his mother's married life, but the telling seemed to be at second hand, and lacked the living touch. I could not help feeling that his treatment of the theme was far behind the reality in vividness and dramatic strength. Now and again he seemed to strike a curious, half-apologetic note, bordering on the sentimental . . . A nonconformist minister whose sermons the mother helped to compose was the foil to the brutal husband. He gave the boy Paul a box of paints, and the mother's heart glowed with pride as she saw her son's budding power . . . It was story-bookish. The elder brother Ernest, whose short career had always seemed to me most moving and dramatic, was not there at all. I was amazed to find there was no mention of him. The character Lawrence called Miriam was in the story, but placed in a bourgeois setting, in the same family from which he later took the Alvina of *The Lost Girl.* He had placed Miriam in this household as a sort of foundling, and it was there that Paul Morel made her acquaintance.

The theme developed into the mother's opposition to Paul's love for Miriam. In this connection several remarks in this first draft impressed me particularly. Lawrence had written: 'What was it he (Paul Morel) wanted of her (Miriam)? Did he want her to break his mother down in him? Was that what he wanted?'

And again: 'Mrs. Morel saw that if Miriam could only win her son's sex sympathy there would be nothing left for her.'

In another place he said: 'Miriam looked upon Paul as a young man tied to his mother's apron-strings.' Finally, referring to the people around Miriam, he said: 'How should they understand her — petty trades-people!' But the issue was left quite unresolved. Lawrence had carried the situation to the point of deadlock and stopped there.

As I read through the manuscript I had before me all the time the vivid picture of the reality. I felt again the tenseness of the conflict, and the impending spiritual clash. So in my reply I told him I was very surprised that he had kept so far from reality in his story; that I thought what had really happened was much more poignant and interesting than the situations he had invented. In particular I was surprised that he had omitted the story of Ernest, which seemed to me vital enough to be worth telling as it actually happened. Finally I suggested that he should write the whole story again, and keep it true to life.

Two considerations prompted me to make these suggestions. First of all I felt that the theme, if treated adequately, had in it the stuff of a magnificent story. It only wanted setting down, and Lawrence possessed the miraculous power of translating the raw material of life into significant form. That was my first reaction to the problem. My deeper thought was that in the doing of it Lawrence might free himself from his strange obsession with his mother. I thought he might be able to work out the theme in the realm of spiritual reality, where alone it could be worked out, and so resolve the conflict in himself. Since he had elected to deal with the big and difficult subject of his family, and the interactions of the various relationships, I felt he ought to do it faithfully — 'with both hands earnestly', as he was fond of quoting. It seemed to me that if he was able to treat the theme with strict integrity he would thereby walk into freedom, and cast off the trammelling past like an old skin.

The particular issue he might give to the story never entered my head. That was of no consequence. The great thing was that I thought I could see a liberated Lawrence coming out of it. Towards Lawrence's mother I had no bitter feeling, and could have none, because she was his mother. But I felt that he was being strangled in a bond that was even more powerful since her death, and that until he was freed from it he was held in check and unable to develop.

In all this I acted from pure intuition, arising out of my deep knowledge of his situation. I said no word of this to him because I thought it must inevitably work itself out in the novel, provided he treated the subject with integrity. And I had a profound faith in Lawrence's fundamental integrity.

He fell in absolutely with my suggestion and asked me to write what I could remember of our early days, because, as he truthfully said, my recollection of those days was so much clearer than his. I agreed to do so, and began almost at once, but had not got very far when word came that Lawrence was dangerously ill with pneumonia. I was sure he would get better and went on writing the notes for him. When he was convalescent the first thing he wrote was a tiny pencilled message to me, saying: 'Did I frighten you all? I'm sorry. Never mind, I'm soon going to be all right.'

I saw him during the Christmas holiday sitting by the fire in his bedroom, grievously thin, but yet somehow so vital. Whenever I looked at him, I seemed to see the naked flame of life. It was so as he sat in his room on that sunny Saturday morning, from time to time putting a scrap of linen to his lips, and then dropping it into the fire. He looked at me with eyes in which a light would leap, then sink, and leap again. I was staying with 'Helen'. Lawrence asked me where we were going for lunch, and in the way he suddenly turned his head when I told him, I saw the whole bitterness of his illness and his enforced severance from activity.

He asked me if I had written the notes I promised to do, and I told him I had begun to write them before he was ill and just went on. He said he was going to Bournemouth as soon as he was strong enough, and after that he would come and fetch them. This was our first real talk since his mother's funeral. Some of the old magic returned, the sense of inner understanding which was the essence of our friendship.

Lawrence wrote from Bournemouth: 'I advise you never to come here for a holiday. The place exists for the sick. They hide the fact as far as possible, but it's like a huge hospital. At every turn you come across invalids being pushed or pulled along. Quite a nice place of course, everything arranged for the comfort of the invalid, sunny sheltered corners and the like, but pah — I shall be glad when I get away.'

He broke the journey home to stay with Edward Garnett and returned to Eastwood early in February. I was told that he was breaking off his engagement to

X. He sent me a postcard: 'I hear you're in digs at the moment. If you are still in digs next week, I'd like to come and see you, if I may.'

After the long absence Lawrence felt nervous at meeting my people. A sudden spurt of wintry weather had made it difficult for me to get home, so I sent him my temporary address, and he came to see me early in the week. He surprisingly brought me a box of chocolates. I could hardly believe that we were really together again. I looked at him from time to time to make sure it was not illusion. He spoke bitterly about his illness and what he considered the cause of it. According to my old custom I did not contradict him but let him talk himself out. I never took his assertions about people and things seriously. They were not necessarily true, but they showed the inclination of his mood. To occupy my nervous hands I had provided myself with some knitting. Lawrence looked at it and said acidly:

'There's nothing I admire like industry,' and I was unable to knit any more.

We tried to pick up the interrupted threads of our friendship. I learned that he was free from his engagement. I felt that now he must have convinced himself, and told him I would not have had things otherwise.

'That's just you,' he said half bitterly; 'select only what is good from an experience and then say that everything happens for the best.'

I could see no reason why all should not happen for

the best, but he seemed full of chagrin and unappeased grief. I wanted his mood of resentment to evaporate, and was about to move over to his side, when, as plainly as though he spoke aloud, there came into my consciousness the words: 'Don't imagine that because mother's dead you can claim me', and I felt the ground taken from under my feet. Lawrence must have been aware of my check, because he roused himself to talk — about the all-embracing nature of the Roman Catholic Church.

After a little while he said:

'If we were to marry now you'd expect me to stay at home.' I replied that naturally I should.

'Home is the place one works in,' I said.

'But I don't want a home,' he said obstinately, 'I want to be free. I think I shall go abroad.'

He said he would go first to Germany and stay in the Rhineland with some relatives of his German uncle, and later go further afield, and remain abroad probably a year. It seemed to me an excellent plan. In the course of a year's wandering abroad I thought he might come to some kind of peace with himself. But he still seemed deeply unsatisfied, with himself, or me, or both of us. He crossed to the hearth and sat there in silence, elbow on knee, his head resting on his hand, staring into the fire. It was the familiar spectacle; Lawrence in the grip of the forces that pulled him with equal power in opposite directions. But what I saw at the moment was his utter loneliness, his separation, as it seemed, from everything else in life; and as always, I was overcome with pity. I slipped my hand into his that was hanging limp . . . This is the meeting Lawrence has commemorated in the poem 'After Many Days'.

I gave him the notes I had written and he subsequently incorporated them into the novel, altering and adapting them to suit his purpose. I went with him to the railway station. On the tram he seized my hand:

'I wish we could run away on this,' he said.

But I did not see why we needed to run away. Then he told me that he would probably never return to school. He was making a little money by his writing and would try to live on it. If the worst should come to the worst he could always go back into school. But he hoped it wouldn't come to that. Down on the platform we were reminded so much of his days in College. He was jubilant at the thought of being free from school:

'For him no more the sitting class shall wait,' he said gleefully.

The writing of the novel (still called *Paul Morel*) now went on apace. Lawrence passed the manuscript on to me as he wrote it, a few sheets at a time, just as he had done with *The White Peacock*, only that this story was written with incomparably greater speed and intensity.

The early pages delighted me. Here was all that spontaneous flow, the seemingly effortless translation of life that filled me with admiration. His descriptions of family life were so vivid, so exact, and so concerned with everyday things we had never even noticed before. There was Mrs. Morel ready for ironing, lightly spitting on the iron to test its heat, invested with a reality and significance hitherto unsuspected. It was his power to transmute the common experiences into significance that I always felt to be Lawrence's greatest gift. He did not distinguish between small and great happenings; the common round was full of mystery, awaiting interpretation. Born and bred of working people, he had the rare gift of seeing them from within, and revealing them on their own plane. An incident that particularly pleased me was where Morel was recovering from an accident at the pit, and his friend Jerry came to see him. The conversation of the two men and their tenderness to one another were a revelation to me. I felt that Lawrence was coming into his true kingdom as a creative artist, and an interpreter of the people to whom he belonged.

I saw him fairly frequently during the first weeks of the writing of *Sons and Lovers*. He went quite often also to my married sister's cottage, where he talked about himself with his customary frankness. He told her: 'A.'s quite ready to step into mother's shoes. If I go to Nottingham in the evening it's — "Where have I been? Whom have I seen? What was my business?" I say to her "Ask me another." A. mustn't think she's mother.'

He came to the farm again, a little shy at meeting father:

'But it will be all right after the first brush,' he said.

Mother gave him the same quiet welcome as ever, but father was not the same. The difference was subtle. There was no longer that indefinable attitude of special recognition on father's part. In treating him as some-one quite ordinary he managed to convey a sense of forfeited regard that Lawrence felt acutely.

But then he was not the same either. The sunny disposition that used to create such a happy atmosphere was seldom in evidence. He was spasmodic and rest-less, resentful of the need to be careful of his health, and not well adapted to fit into the rather grim mid-lands life now that he had no mother to make a home for him. In company he would maintain his jaunty exterior, but below the surface was a hopelessness hardly to be distinguished from despair. He seemed like a man with a broken mainspring. With all his gifts, he was somehow cut off, unable to attain that complete participation in life that he craved for.

There was a Sunday when he came to the farm to tea. After tea we stood round the piano singing hymns and Folk songs. My younger sister, who was playing the piano, turned to the hymn: 'We are but little children weak'. I was about to turn the page, saying, 'We don't want that,' but Lawrence stopped me impulsively.

'It's true, we *are*. Let's have it,' and he joined in the singing with gusto.

Later he watched my brothers getting ready to go out.

'Are you going courting?' he asked them, half enviously.

'We're supposed to be,' they replied, laughing at his strange question.

When we were alone his painfully bright manner fell from him.

'Except in relation to beauty or passion you never think of sex,' he said to me. We talked about his writing and he upbraided me for not making an effort to do something myself. He was so sure I could write if I would try. 'If you had only two books out, I shouldn't care,' he said. I knew he was reproaching himself for having occupied my time with his own work. Presently he said in a halting way, as if struggling to find the exact words:

'When we are not together, since I have been away from you, I don't think the same, feel the same; I'm not the same man. *I* can't write poetry.'

The words went to my heart, for his tone was the extreme of sincerity and of despair. We were together again, and outwardly there was nothing to keep us apart, but his mother's ban was more powerful now than in her lifetime. I began to realize that whatever approach Lawrence made to me inevitably involved him in a sense of disloyalty to his mother. Some bond, some understanding, most likely unformulated and all the stronger for that, seemed to exist between them. It was a bond that definitely excluded me from the only position in which I could be of vital help to him. We were back in the old dilemma, but it was a thousand times more cruel because of the altered circumstances. He seemed to be fixed in the centre of the tension, helpless, waiting for one pull to triumph over the other.

The novel was written in this state of spirit, at a white heat of concentration. The writing of it was fundamentally a terrific fight for a bursting of the tension. The break came in the treatment of Miriam. As the sheets of manuscript came rapidly to me I was bewildered and dismayed at that treatment. I began to perceive that I had set Lawrence a task far beyond his strength. In my confidence I had not doubted that he would work out the problem with integrity. But he burked the real issue. It was his old inability to face his problem squarely. His mother had to be supreme, and for the sake of that supremacy every disloyalty was permissible.

The realization of this slowly dawned on me as I read the manuscript. He asked for my opinion, but comment seemed futile — not merely futile, but impossible. I could not appeal to Lawrence for justice as between his treatment of Mrs. Morel and Miriam. He left off coming to see me and sent the manuscript by post. His avoidance of me was significant. I felt it was useless to attempt to argue the matter out with him. Either he was aware of what he was doing and persisted, or he did not know, and in that case no amount of telling would enlighten him. It was one of the things he had to find out for himself. The baffling truth, of course, lay between the two. He was aware, but he was under the spell of the domination that had ruled his life hitherto, and he refused to know. So instead of a release and a deliverance from bondage, the bondage was glorified and made absolute. His mother conquered indeed, but the vanquished one was her son. In *Sons and Lovers* Lawrence handed his mother the laurels of victory.

The Clara of the second half of the story was a clever adaptation of elements from three people, and her creation arose as a complement to Lawrence's mood of failure and defeat. The events related had no foundation in fact, whatever their psychological significance. Having utterly failed to come to grips with his problem in real life, he created the imaginary Clara as a compensation. Even in the novel the compensation is unreal and illusory, for at the end Paul Morel calmly hands her back to her husband, and remains suspended over the abyss of his despair. Many of the incidents struck me as cheap and commonplace, in spite of the hard brilliance of the narration. I realized that I had naively credited Lawrence with superhuman powers of detachment.

The shock of *Sons and Lovers* gave the death-blow

to our friendship. If I had told Lawrence that I had died before, I certainly died again. I had a strange feeling of separation from the body. The daily life was sheer illusion. The only reality was the betrayal of *Sons and Lovers*. I felt it was a betrayal in an inner sense, for I had always believed that there was a bond between us, if it was no more than the bond of a common suffering. But the brutality of his treatment seemed to deny any bond. That I understood so well what made him do it only deepened my despair. He had to present a distorted picture of our association so that the martyr's halo might sit becomingly on his mother's brow. But to give a recognizable picture of our friendship which yet completely left out the years of devotion to the development of his genius — devotion that had been pure joy — seemed to me like presenting *Hamlet* without the Prince of Denmark. What else but the devotion to a common end had held us together against his mother's repeated assaults? Neither could I feel that he had represented in any degree faithfully the nature and quality of our desperate search for a right relationship. I was hurt beyond all expression. I didn't know how to bear it.

Lawrence had said that he never took sides; but his attitude placed him tacitly on the side of those who had mocked at love — except mother-love. He seemed to have identified himself with the prevailing atmosphere of ridicule and innuendo. It was a fatal alignment, for it made me see him as a philistine of the philistines, and not, as I had always believed, inwardly honouring an unspoken bond, and suffering himself from the strange hostility to love. He had sometimes argued — in an effort to convince himself — that morality and art have nothing to do with one another. However that might be, I could not help feeling that integrity and art have a great deal to do with one another. The best I could think of him was that he had run with the hare and hunted with the hounds . . . His significance withered and his dimensions shrank. He ceased to matter supremely.

I tried hard to remind myself that after all *Sons and Lovers* was only a novel. It was not the truth, although it must inevitably stand for truth. I could hear in advance Lawrence's protesting voice: 'Of course it isn't the truth. It isn't meant for the truth. It's an adaptation from life, as all art must be. It *isn't* what I think of you; you know it isn't. What shall I put? What do you want me to put . . .?' in a mounting crescendo of irritation and helplessness. I felt that words could only exacerbate the situation. The remedy must be left to time. And as I sat and looked at the subtle distortion of what had been the deepest values of my life, the one gleam of light was the realization that Lawrence had overstated his case; that some day his epic of maternal love and filial devotion would be viewed from another angle, that of his own final despair.

The book was written in about six weeks, under the influence of something amounting almost to frenzy.

Although he avoided me Lawrence wanted to know what I thought of the novel. So, after I had studied the last sheets of the manuscript, I suggested that, as I had a holiday on a certain Monday in March, I should spend the week-end with my sister and we might meet and talk about the book. Lawrence replied that he had promised to go on a visit to a schoolmaster friend in Staffordshire on that particular week-end, but he would try to get back in good time on the Sunday. From the tone of his letter I judged that he intended me to have an opportunity of saying anything I wished to say, but it was to be a limited opportunity. I made some notes on minor points and took the manuscript with me.

Lawrence liked the atmosphere of my sister's cottage. Her husband's genial presence, and her own quick intuitive likes and dislikes, coupled with an equally quick sympathy, made a setting in which he could feel entirely at home. He entertained them by his tales of people he had met in literary circles. With his gift for mimicry he would reproduce comic incidents and bring them to tears of laughter. He painted a droll picture of himself and another young poet walking through London at midnight with a tipsy and amorous woman-poet, old enough to be their mother, whose harp they were carrying . . . Lawrence's tales doubtless lost nothing in the telling.

It was his ambition to make my brother-in-law drunk, or at least to 'loosen his tongue', and with that end in view he brought a bottle of wine to the cottage. The two men drank together, carefully watching the effect upon each other, but while Lawrence grew slightly hilarious his companion became glum and his mouth shut tight. The wine only sealed his lips.

Lawrence told them how Edward Garnett and he had drunk wine together, and added quaintly:

'Garnett wanted to make me talk, but I always knew what I was saying. He thinks I told him everything, but I didn't. I told him nearly everything. But there were some things I didn't tell him.'

We awaited Lawrence on the Sunday with mixed anticipations. My sister knew nothing about the novel. I had long ago formed the habit of keeping my own counsel, and she had the supreme wisdom of never asking questions. Lawrence had said he might by luck be with us for the midday meal, as the one train of the day set off in the morning, but he failed to put in an appearance. The afternoon wore on. My brother-in-law and I went for a run on our bicycles, but Lawrence had not arrived at tea-time. It began to rain, and just as dusk was drawing in he appeared at the door, white and exhausted, carrying a heavy suitcase. He had been travelling all day and was nearly worn out with the cross-country journey from the Staffordshire border. The trains had been slow and the connections bad. In addition there was a touring theatrical party on the train and the transfer of their 'properties' had occasioned no little delay. Finally Lawrence had walked up the long hill from the station having had very little to eat during the day. I lifted the suitcase and exclaimed at its weight.

'I haven't got a couple of suits in it,' he snapped savagely. I had never heard him speak in that tone before.

My sister put out tea for him and he took his boots off. They set him in the armchair, 'the grandfather's chair', and presently we drew round the fire. But Lawrence's nerves were frayed. The long journey had tired him, and at heart he was disappointed that he had arrived so late. He kept up his jaunty air, however, telling us about the 'theatricals' and their 'properties'. They had amused him at first. He had thought travelling along with them great fun. He had mixed with the party and talked to them, but as the day dragged on he had found them boring. Now he could only keep his disappointment in check by an effort. I stooped to prop his boots up against the fender so that they should dry the better. He apparently thought I was going to push them out of the way and turned on me a look of sudden fury. When he saw his mistake he swung his head round quickly. My sister and her husband understood his mood of chagrin and humoured him like a sick child. They laughed at his little sallies, accompanied by mimicry, about the theatrical party until he tired of the subject. Then he fell to talking about his friend who had married not long before and had got a baby son.

'Fatherhood's a myth,' Lawrence declared. 'There's nothing in it. I asked — how he felt about it, and he said he felt nothing, nothing at all. He has no feeling whatever towards that infant. There's no such thing as fatherhood,' he concluded slowly, as though the words tasted sweet on his tongue.

My sister and I were silent. Lawrence's perversity was no new thing to us. We were acquainted with the history of the young man in question, and could not help reflecting that his fatherhood involved someone's motherhood, a myth less easily disposed of. Lawrence knew quite well what we were thinking, and enlarged upon the theme characteristically. 'The average man with a family,' he went on, 'is nothing but a cart-horse, dragging the family behind him for the best part of his life. I'm not going to be a cart-horse.'

My brother-in-law twinkled at him, chuckling softly.

'You're nothing but a rake, Bert, a positive rake,' he said.

'Nay, dunna say that, Bill, dunna say that,' Lawrence replied comically.

The evening passed in talk that had an acid flavour under its lightness, and when he took his departure his fundamental desolation showed palpably beneath his flippant exterior.

He came next day in the early afternoon, tense, looking as if he had not slept. Almost at once he asked my sister to give him a cup of tea. He had a headache. He had stayed in bed late, but still felt tired. We sat in the cottage, talking about nothing in particular, and the precious minutes slipped by. Lawrence looked far too much a sick man for me to dream of telling him all I thought and felt about his novel. I knew that he dreaded what I might say, yet he wanted to know. At least he did not want it to be said that he had given me no opportunity to speak. I made no move until he looked at me with an interrogative glance, and said:

'Do you want to go out, or would you rather stay in?'

I said it depended upon how he felt, and he declared he felt all right.

We went out into the cloudy afternoon and walked past Greasley Church, then took the footpath through the fields where he and my brothers had worked together at hay harvest. Lawrence kept a sharp look-out for violets in the hedgerows. He said there must be some about because A. had seen youths coming home from the pit with bunches of violets and celandines in their hands. At the mention of violets and celandines I had hard work to keep the tears back, because it seemed as if springtime and spring flowers had gone out of my life for ever. Until then his manner had been bleak and forbidding, but now he softened a little and said almost wistfully:

'I thought perhaps you would have something to say about the writing.'

I felt as if I was sinking in deep water. But it was now the eleventh hour, and the time for speaking had gone by, and I merely said:

'I've put some notes in with the manuscript,' and he replied quietly, as though he was suddenly out of breath, 'Oh, all right. I thought you might like to say something. That's all.'

It was not that I would not speak but simply that I could not. Between pride and anguish I found it impossible to tell him that the account he had given of our friendship amounted to a travesty of the real thing. His defensive attitude had kept me at bay, as he intended it should, and now the time was gone. It was too late. I could only remain silent. We spoke no more about the novel and soon turned back towards the cottage.

Lawrence's manner at tea showed a marked difference. He was freed from some kind of apprehension. An acute alertness was visible to me beneath his flippant conversation. He was puzzled and was watching me narrowly, trying to find a clue to the situation. I had no clue to give him, and felt offended at the hard quality of his observation. It was time for me to return home. I knew that he would walk some of the way with me and I suddenly turned to my sister and asked her to accompany us. She looked from Lawrence to me in perplexity.

'Do you really want me?' she asked.

'I was thinking you'd be company for Bert on the way home,' I replied in a casual tone.

Lawrence did not speak. I was standing in front of the mirror that hung over the mantelpiece, pinning on my hat, and my eyes met his fixed upon me in a look of intense concentration. His stare sent a revulsion of feeling through me. He seemed a total stranger.

I gave him the parcel of manuscript. He put it ready to take in a fatalistic silence, and the three of us set out. Lawrence insisted on pushing my bicycle, although I begged him to let me take it. He said he felt he would never want to get on a bicycle again, but he didn't mind how many miles he walked. My sister and I walked together on the footpath, and Lawrence was a little step away on the road. It was not easy to talk to him there, so he walked for most of the way in silence. At the top of the hill he said he would turn back, he was tired. I got on my bicycle and rode home, feeling numbed to the core, for I knew that in our wordless way we had come to an end. I had nourished a faint hope that our little time together might yield an opportunity for a real discussion. But Lawrence was expecting me to attack him. He knew I must be hurt, and thought I should be furiously angry. What he did not understand was that the hurt went deeper than any anger. It went down to the roots of my feeling for him and altered my conception of his nature.

He walked back to the cottage with my sister. She told me later that he said, referring to me:

'She's wild with me, isn't she? She's angry about something.' My sister replied that she was not aware of it, but he refused to believe her, and insisted:

'She is, she's angry. Hasn't she told you about it?'

He seemed tired and dejected, she said. When they reached the cottage he took the manuscript and said he would go home to bed.

There was no further attempt at discussion of the novel. Lawrence made no approach to me nor I to him. I returned what few books of his I had, and he replied in a casual note. The more I thought about the situation — and it was impossible to think about anything else — the more certain I became of the futility of attempting to reason the matter out with him. I realized that the entire structure of the story rested upon the attitude he had adopted. To do any kind of justice to our relationship would involve a change in his attitude towards his mother's influence, and of that I was now convinced he was incapable. It was the old situation in a new setting, the necessity for the mother's supremacy. More than a year before he had told me so in exact words, only without referring directly to his mother:

'You are the irremediable thing,' he had said, looking at me as though he would consume me with his eyes. 'You are what *has* to be. You are what cannot be helped. The great thing now is that you should not become bitter.'

It roused my irony that he should take my doom for granted, and in spite of my misery I laughed, and replied·

'No, ı don't think I shall turn bitter.' But Lawrence was in such deadly earnest he did not perceive why I laughed. Now, in the novel, he had taken up the same position, and appointed himself judge and executioner. He held over me a doom of negation and futility. It pressed upon me like a weight, making the nights and days a torture. I dreaded lest I should come to fulfil it, as he seemed convinced I must.

My next meeting with Lawrence came about by pure chance. On Easter Monday I was in the booking-hall of the railway station waiting for my sister, when suddenly Lawrence appeared at the barrier, accompanied by his sister and her fiancé. I had a view of Lawrence for a full moment before he was aware of my presence. The misery I saw depicted in his face was beyond anything I had ever imagined. Utterly lonely, he looked as if his life had turned to complete negation. His expression at that moment was the direct development of the face that he used to turn towards the dark fields when he would declare, in agony of frustration: '*Nothing* matters.' His look changed the moment he caught sight of me, but it was still a joyless face. I explained why I was there. We talked for a few minutes, and then he went with his companions to an afternoon show at the Empire. Lawrence told my sister of the brief encounter. He said that I looked white, but perhaps I was cold.

My sister has told me that in those days Lawrence impressed her with a sense of his divine belief in himself. She said he seemed to feel he was important to the world, and he resented any claim that would curtail his experience and therefore his usefulness. He felt himself a medium charged with some power for the good of mankind. Yet he wished he could escape it and grow stout, and attractive to women. He longed to be loved as a man instead of as a poet. He told her also that he was a common man with an intellect, and that I was in love with his intellect . . . He would say one day that he must accept every experience that came to him, for the sake of his 'mission', and the next that he was nothing but a simple, ordinary man, with a little more than the ordinary man's mental equipment. Her final verdict on him was: 'He sees the light and chooses the dark.'

I saw Lawrence for the next and last time on a Sunday morning some three weeks later when father and I drove to my sister's cottage. I did not know that Lawrence was spending the week-end there, but I was not surprised to see him. We arrived unexpectedly and I could not help seeing that my coming startled him. He looked a different man from the one I had seen momentarily at the barrier of the railway station. The look of despair was gone. He appeared more ordinary and equable. But for once I saw Lawrence tongue-tied. He didn't know what to say to us. He went outside and sat on the low garden wall, leaning forward and looking intently at the ground, in an odd attitude of concentration. Presently he came into the cottage and looked at me curiously as though he would ask whether I had brought him some message. I asked him if he would care to drive home with us. He said he would like to, only my sister was expecting him to stay. So, true to his habit of letting other people make his decisions, he left it with her, and she, having prepared for him, naturally preferred that he should stay. But he drove part of the way with us. He almost winced at my father's casual tone, so different from the warmth of old days.

Lawrence talked to us with a forced brightness about his going to Germany. He expected to go within a few days. I asked about his work, and he spoke of a play that was perhaps going to be produced in London. On the level above Watnall hill he got out of the trap to return by the footpath over the fields. We shook hands and said good-bye like casual acquaintances, and father hoped he would manage to keep in better health. Lawrence thanked him. Before we disappeared round a bend in the road I turned and saw him still standing where he had alighted, looking after us. I waved my hand and he raised his hat with the familiar gesture. I never saw him again.

My sister said later that he returned to the cottage in a thoughtful mood. He carved the joint, and was subdued and gentle. In the afternoon he and her husband were lying out in the field on rugs, and Lawrence suddenly exclaimed:

'Bill, I like a *gushing* woman.'

On a Sunday evening soon after his departure for Germany, Lawrence's sister E. paid an unexpected call on my sister. In the course of conversation she remarked:

'Our Bert can never love any woman. He could only love his mother.'

The remark rang like the echo of a family discussion.

It was not long before I had a postcard from Lawrence, a beautiful view of Trier Cathedral. In another week or so came a letter in which he said: 'I am going through *Paul Morel*. I'm sorry it turned out as it has. You'll have to go on forgiving me.'

His words aroused no response in me. My forgiveness or non-forgiveness was equally irrelevant. What mattered was something in himself, something he had to find out, which only the inexorable logic of circumstance could show him. As for myself, I felt that I had suffered a terrible inner injury. It required all my effort to avoid a collapse.

A further letter arrived from Lawrence a few weeks later. It was addressed to me, and enclosed within a descriptive letter for the family to read was another, which was inscribed: *Pour vous seulement*. It contained a hysterical announcement of the new attachment he had formed, and enjoined the strictest secrecy upon me: 'Don't tell M., don't tell N.C., don't tell *anybody*. Only A. knows . . .' I felt it was probably the last request Lawrence would ever make of me, and I kept his secret.

The news came as a shock, but I was not really surprised. My deepest feeling was a sense of relief. At last I was really free. I had always felt a great responsibility towards Lawrence. This now vanished. He had passed definitely beyond my ken. Now I understood what he had meant when, not many weeks earlier, he had said to me in a querulous voice:

'Are you *great* enough?'

My inveterate irony had prompted me to reply: 'Probably not.'

I answered his letter immediately: 'Your news does not surprise me. I half expected it. In my heart I am glad, because it sets me free.' All the same, the realization that our long, and in many ways wonderful friendship had actually come to an end was a very deep blow, comparable to a kind of death. I had no illusions about it. In the passing of Lawrence I saw also the extinction of my greater self. Life without him had a bleak aspect. I had grown up within his orbit, and now that he was definitely gone I had to make a difficult new beginning. For a long time in a quiet and deliberate way I wished I had done with life. The remnant that was left looked so ugly.

It was then that I happened to find *The Brothers Karamazov* in our library. I was quite unable to read. Before my eyes had travelled half way down the page my mind refused to take in the sense. I found myself gazing at the printed words and seeing only the wreckage of my life . . . But Dostoevsky's masterpiece gripped my attention. I took it home, and the book completely absorbed me, mercifully shutting out my own disaster. I was fascinated immediately by the psychological plan, setting out the whole psychic panorama with such economy. The terrible old man and his four sons, each by a different mother, provided at once that clash of the spirit that was for me the real substance of drama. In some incomprehensible way I seemed to have known all the characters before. The saintly Zosima was no stranger . . . There were times when, like Ivan Karamazov, I wanted to give in my ticket, but Alyosha's murmured: 'It is disobedience', spoke to something deep within me. And the story of the *Grand Inquisitor* was a problem to turn over in one's soul to the end of life . . . I don't know how long I kept the book. I seemed to be reading it for months. Probably I read many parts of it several times. When at last I reluctantly returned it to the library I felt that I had been living in another world. Its effect upon me was exactly analogous to deep sleep in illness. It had placed a distance between me and the catastrophe of life. I left it refreshed in spirit.

I was now able to face my own inner chaos. In the terrible necessity to understand what had really happened between Lawrence and me I set myself to analyse our friendship. I unravelled it strand by strand, and somehow managed to get an objective view, so that I was able to go forward into life instead of being crushed under a dead weight of unassimilated experience.

Lawrence had not replied to my letter telling him I was glad to feel myself set free, and in the following spring his first book of poems was published. A copy came to me from the publisher — with the author's compliments. These were for the most part the poems that Lawrence had written in the thick little college notebook that I knew so well. Very few of the pieces were new to me. I was glad to receive the book, so I asked my sister for his address, and wrote, thanking him for it, and made a few remarks about the poems. His reply, and also a bulky parcel of proof-sheets, came several days later. I felt that my comments were unwelcome, for Lawrence wrote: 'I think the little poetry book is all right . . . I'm sending you the proofs of the novel, I think you ought to see it before it's published. I heard from A. that you were in digs. again. Send the novel on to her when you've done with it [here he gave her address]. This last year hasn't been all roses for me. I've had my ups and my downs out here with Frieda. But we mean to marry as soon as the divorce is through. We shall settle down quite quietly somewhere, probably in Berkshire. Frieda and I discuss you endlessly. We should like you to come out to us some time, if you would care to. But we are leaving here in about a week, it's getting too hot for us, I mean the weather, not the place. I must leave off now, they're waiting for me. . . .'

I read his letter several times, not knowing whether to laugh or to cry. I felt suffocated. The clumsiness of his approach was plain, but to my mind there was a priggish note as well. It was the tone of the letter that offended me. There was the off-handed attempt to be casual and matter-of-fact, and yet to appeal to my sympathy. I wondered also why he should send his novel to me in this manner, as though I was a stranger to it. I knew it far too well to have any desire to read it again. Indeed, I didn't dare to risk a second reading, for I was by no means sure of my capacity to recover a second time. I did glance through some pages, however, hoping that in the interval his outlook might have mellowed and led him to soften some harshness. But I found both story and mood alike unchanged.

As chance would have it, my sister came to see me, and in my dismay I did what I had never done before; I showed her Lawrence's letter. She was furious.

'How dare he send a letter like this to *you*,' she moaned. Then her anger flashed out: 'Send it back to him,' she said. 'Send it back.' I laughed mirthlessly.

'Oh, I've had worse letters than this from him,' I said.

'Then some others ought to have gone back before this,' she retorted.

I showed her the proofs of the novel and suggested

that she should take it to read. But she would have
nothing to do with it. I didn't want it either, so I
reversed the wrapper and posted the proofs as Lawrence
had directed.

The suggestion that I should return Lawrence's
letter struck me at first as wild and impossible. But I
turned the idea over in my mind, and the more I
looked at it, the better I liked it. I shrank from doing
what seemed a brutal thing, yet I felt that the action in
itself would say effectively what no words could say.
One thing seemed certain; there was no possible basis
for any future friendship, whereas the stage was set for
the most grotesque misunderstanding. I felt that the
time had come for a break, and a clean break seemed
infinitely preferable. Another motive had some weight
with me. On the occasion when his mother made her
final intervention between us, immediately before her
fatal illness, some words Lawrence had used in the long
harangue with which he sought to justify his action to
himself remained in my mind. He had said:

'An ounce of justice is worth a ton of generosity.
Any woman will give a man a ton of generosity, but is
there a woman who will give him an ounce of justice?'

I could not refrain from thinking:

'Here is your ounce of justice.'

All the same, I hated to hurt him. But I copied out
the foreign address and put his letter — which was torn
a little through being unfolded so many times — in the
envelope. As I dropped it in the pillar box I felt sorry

for him. I knew it would give him a shock. And later, when I thought the letter had probably reached him, I was grieved to think of his pain. But I was not sorry for my action. It was somehow necessary. Indeed, I never did regret it, for it acted as a kind of release and let out all feeling of resentment. No words could have produced such a cleansing effect. In a favourite phrase of Lawrence's, it drew the line under the finished sum. Not that I felt the sum to be entirely finished. I thought it was just possible that he would write and say he hadn't meant to be so stupid. But he never wrote to me again, and I never really wished him to, nor did I ever write to him. I had gone with him as far as I could go. Nothing further was possible.

In the days when the cloud of his mother's disapproval first began to loom heavy over our young horizon, Lawrence said to me, 'Of course, it will be *you* who will write my epitaph.'

I was too pained and startled to speak, and answered only with a shake of the head. He smiled at me brilliantly and reiterated softly, nodding:

'Oh yes, you will. It will fall to you to write my epitaph.'

And from time to time in moments of intense feeling he would repeat his strange forecast. His words had no literal meaning for me then, because in those days Lawrence and death seemed to stand at opposite poles. He was always to me a symbol of overflowing life. He